Joseph Griffiths Swayne

Obstetric aphorisms for the use of students commencing midwifery practice

Joseph Griffiths Swayne

Obstetric aphorisms for the use of students commencing midwifery practice

ISBN/EAN: 9783337713997

Printed in Europe, USA, Canada, Australia, Japan

Cover: Foto ©ninafisch / pixelio.de

More available books at **www.hansebooks.com**

OBSTETRIC APHORISMS

FOR THE

USE OF STUDENTS

COMMENCING

MIDWIFERY PRACTICE

BY

JOSEPH GRIFFITHS SWAYNE, M.D.

CONSULTING PHYSICIAN ACCOUCHEUR TO THE BRISTOL GENERAL HOSPITAL
AND LECTURER ON OBSTETRIC MEDICINE AT THE BRISTOL MEDICAL SCHOOL

Ninth Edition

PHILADELPHIA
P. BLAKISTON, SON, & CO.
1012, WALNUT STREET
1888

PREFACE.

The object of this work is to give the student a few brief and practical directions respecting the management of ordinary cases of labour; and also to point out to him, in extraordinary cases, when and how he may act upon his own responsibility, and when he ought to send for assistance. It has been undertaken by the Author in accordance with a wish often expressed to him by his pupils, and is founded upon his experience of the wants of those who are commencing midwifery practice. The student is never placed in a more trying situation, nor has to incur a greater amount of responsibility, than when he is attending a difficult case of labour in a place remote from medical aid; and the end of this work will be fully answered if it serve to keep any, who may be so situated, from the opposite extremes of temerity or timidity.* It is not intended to be used, in any way, as a substitute for a systematic treatise on midwifery, and therefore many details in anatomy, physiology, pathology, and treatment have been purposely omitted.

It will be observed, that the student is advised to send for assistance whenever it is necessary to use instruments or to introduce the hand into the uterus for the purpose of turning, &c.; and, indeed, in all cases which are necessarily dangerous, and accompanied with more than ordinary difficulty. The diagnosis of such cases is, it is hoped, given at sufficient length to enable him to know when he ought to send for aid; but the treatment is indicated in as few words as possible, because a fuller account of it would cause this book to exceed the limits of a work which is merely intended to serve the temporary purpose of a guide to beginners in the Obstetric art.

---

* For instance, the student who undertakes a case of placenta prævia without sending for assistance, is an example of one extreme; and the student who sends for help to remove a detached placenta from the vagina, of the other.

The Author has only to add, that he feels most grateful for the favourable manner in which the former editions of his work have been received, especially amongst the junior members of the profession. In the present edition he has done his best to improve on the preceding, although in a manual consisting of short and well-established rules for practice there is not the same room for additions and alterations as in a larger work of more theoretical character. Nevertheless, it will be found that, besides several minor alterations, some important additions have been made to the text of the present work, especially in relation to antiseptic midwifery and the mechanism of the third stage of labour.

In many parts of this work the Author has had to refer to some of the absurd notions and ignorant prejudices of midwives and monthly nurses. His remarks, however, on this head, are applicable to a class which was very prevalent when the first edition was published, but not to the well-instructed and certificated midwives and nurses of the present day.

CONTENTS.

PART I.

THE MANAGEMENT OF ORDINARY LABOUR . . . PAGE 1

PART II.

CASES WHICH THE STUDENT MAY UNDERTAKE WITHOUT ASSISTANCE 37

PART III.

CASES IN WHICH THE STUDENT OUGHT TO SEND FOR ASSISTANCE 106

OBSTETRIC APHORISMS.

PART I.

THE MANAGEMENT OF ORDINARY LABOUR.

Importance of Prompt Attendance.

1. WHEN sent for to a labour, obey the call immediately; for then, if you are too early, you can return home until wanted; and if you are too late, it is not your fault.

Delay may occasion—1, various accidents to both mother and child, from sudden delivery without assistance; 2, the loss of the best opportunity for rectifying mal-presentation; 3, the loss of the patient's confidence in you, and the substitution of another practitioner.

Instruments and Medicines which may be required.

2. You may take with you a stethoscope, and also a pocket case containing blunt-pointed scissors, a silver or gum-elastic female catheter, curved needles, silver wire or silk for sutures, ergot of rye, laudanum, oil of turpentine, and sal volatile, or ether.

With the exception of scissors none of these things will be wanted in an ordinary labour; but it is right to be provided with them against emergencies. Cases containing them may be procured at any surgical-instrument maker's shop.

The needles and sutures will be necessary, if the perineum be lacerated. (See 73, Part II.) Hagedorn's needles, No. 6, with quarter-circle curve, are the best.

It is a good plan to carry ergot, both in the form of fresh powder and tincture, in case, as often happens, one of these preparations should prove to be inefficient.

The Extractum Ergotæ Liquidum of the British Pharmacopœia can, however, be depended on in most instances.

Oil of turpentine is not usually carried in a pocket-case; but the author has found it of great efficacy in uterine hæmorrhage.

Preliminary Observations.

3. On first seeing your patient, do not abruptly question her respecting her symptoms, but converse on some ordinary topic, and whilst thus engaged, notice any indications of pain in her countenance, the tone of her voice, or the character of her respiration.

A brusque, abrupt manner of putting questions may flurry a patient so as to cause her pains to be suspended for a considerable period.

In general, the first stage of labour is characterized by low complaints, and an absence of voluntary effort; and the second stage by deep inspirations, a loud outcry, and strong exertions of the voluntary muscles; and thus an attentive observer may form a rough estimate of the progress of a labour.

Questions respecting Pregnancy, Previous Labours, &c.

4. Before making more special inquiries, you may ask respecting the patient's constitution and state of

health during pregnancy, and (if she be not a primipara) the number and character of her previous labours.

A knowledge of these circumstances may enable you to calculate the duration of the present labour, or to anticipate the occurrence of difficulties or complications requiring the assistance of art. For instance, if a woman of middle age be in labour for the first time, a lingering labour may in general be expected; or if it has been necessary in all the previous labours to deliver by instruments, or, if post-partum hæmorrhage has regularly occurred, you may expect similar untoward events in the present labour. As Dr. Lusk well remarks: "The attitude of the medical attendant should be one of watchful expectancy."

Questions respecting the Present Labour.

5. The questions to be asked respecting the present labour are—when the pains were first felt, and where (*e.g.*, whether in the back or abdomen), their character, duration, and frequency; and, last but not least, whether they have been attended with any "show" or discharge of mucus tinged with blood.

A consideration of all these particulars will assist you in ascertaining whether the pains are genuine, and whether the labour has actually commenced.

The "show" denotes the opening of the os uteri, and is one of the most certain signs of commencing labour; it is therefore made of much account by nurses.

How to propose a Vaginal Examination.

6. The only certain information, however, respecting a labour, is derived from a vaginal examination, which should be made as soon as possible, provided the pains

are at all regular. You accordingly signify to the patient, either directly or through the nurse, that you wish her to lie down on the bed, so that you may be able to try the next pain, and inform her as to the progress of the labour.

If your patient shows an unreasonable reluctance to submit to an examination, you may tell her that, for all you know, the labour may be going on very badly, and that you will not be answerable for the result; by thus working upon her fears you will seldom fail to obtain compliance with your request.

How to make a Vaginal Examination.

7. In order to make a vaginal examination, direct the woman to lie on the right side of the bed, but upon her *left* side, with the knees drawn up towards the abdomen; sit down behind her, and pass the forefinger of the right hand (previously anointed with oil or vaseline) into the genital fissure close to the perineum; then direct the finger first backwards towards the lower part of the sacrum, and then upwards and forwards towards the pubis, so as to reach the os uteri, and presenting part of the child. If the os uteri is high up and far back, the fore and middle fingers of the left hand may be substituted for the right forefinger, because they more readily follow the curve of the sacrum.

Amongst the lower classes, women usually wear their ordinary clothes until the labour is over, when they are undressed and put to bed.

Vaginal examinations and other necessary manipulations are to be made beneath the clothes of the patient, whose person should be in no way exposed.

After examining, the fingers should be wiped in a napkin provided for the purpose, and placed beneath the bed-clothes.

It is as well to caution a beginner against passing his finger into the anterior part of the genital fissure, as, by so doing, he may fail to find the entrance of the vagina, puzzle himself very much, and annoy the patient, who may thus discover that she has been intrusted to a very young hand.

If the fore and middle fingers of the left hand are used, they should be introduced as the forefinger of the right hand is being withdrawn.

When to Examine.

8. In general, it is better to examine during a pain; but an examination, to be complete, should be made both during and after a pain; during a pain (if the labour be in the first stage) it should be strictly limited to the os uteri, vagina, and surrounding parts. When the pain is over, and not until then, the finger may be passed through the os uteri, in order to examine the presentation.

Any attempt to make out the presentation when the membranes are rendered tense during a pain, will in all probability cause their rupture, an accident always to be avoided in the first stage of labour, especially if the presentation be at all unfavourable. (See Part III., 15 and 19.) When the pain is over, the membranes and os uteri become flaccid, and the presentation is much more easily distinguished.

Information derived from Examination.

9. The information derived from a vaginal examination is very complete, for by it you learn,—
i. Whether the passages are in proper condition for

labour. ii. Whether labour has actually commenced. iii. Whether it is in the first or second stage. iv. Whether the presentation is natural. v. Whether you can leave your patient for a time with safety.

State of Passages, &c.

10. i. When the passages are in a proper condition for labour, the pelvis is roomy, with the os uteri in its centre; both the os and vagina are soft, dilatable, moister than usual, and sometimes plentifully bedewed with mucus: the canal of the vagina is neither encroached upon by the rectum and its contents behind, nor by the bladder in front; its walls are rugose in primiparæ, but much smoother in multiparæ, especially at its upper extremity, where its calibre is also greater; its temperature is not raised, nor is it tender under an ordinary examination.

In a pelvis of normal dimensions, the shortest diameter should not be less than four inches, and it should be impossible to touch the upper part of the sacrum with the finger, in an ordinary examination.

In multiparæ, the os uteri is usually situated more anteriorly than in primiparæ, in whom it is sometimes so high up and far back, at the commencement of labour, that it is scarcely possible to reach it, unless you examine with two fingers of the left hand.

With respect to the mucous secretion, Wigand remarks that "the more albuminous it is the better, and it is always a good sign when lumps of albuminous matter come away from time to time; the thicker, softer, and more cushiony the os uteri is, the more mucus does it secrete.

Signs of Commencing Labour.

11. ii. Labour is known to have actually commenced by the occurrence of pains, which return at regular intervals, and increase in frequency and force, and which, on making a vaginal examination, are found to be attended with a mucous show, and to have caused more or less dilatation of the os uteri.

During the ninth month of pregnancy, the uterus usually sinks somewhat in the abdomen, and this subsidence, while it relieves the respiratory organs, causes pressure upon the rectum, bladder, and other contents of the pelvis, occasioning frequent desire to pass water and go to stool; these symptoms are so usual, that they have been considered as premonitory signs of labour.

In multiparæ, the os uteri is sometimes so open before the actual commencement of labour as to admit the tip of the index finger, and even to allow the presentation to be distinguished.

In primiparæ, it is usually closed until labour has actually begun.

Signs of First Stage.

12. iii. *a.* The first stage of labour is occupied in the dilatation of the os uteri. This process is effected solely by the contractions of the uterus, unaided by any of the voluntary muscles. It is characterized by peculiar cutting or grinding pains, first felt in the back, and gradually extending to the front.

State of Os Uteri, &c., in First Stage.

b. On making a vaginal examination, you can feel that the upper part of the vagina is occupied by a soft, rounded tumour, formed by the lower portion of the uterus. (*Fig.* 1.) In the centre of this is the circular aperture of the os tincæ, dilated to the size of a sixpence, shilling, half-crown, crown, or even larger;

Fig. 1.

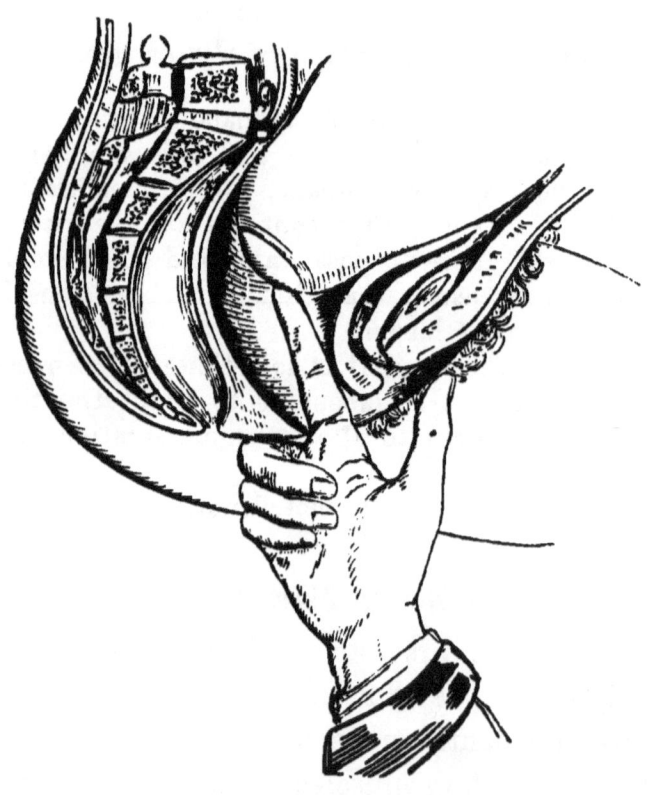

and within the os can be felt the membranous bag of the waters containing the presenting part of the child. When a pain comes on, the os uteri becomes thin and tense; the bag of the waters, which was before flaccid, becomes globular and tense as a drum, and protrudes more or less through the os, which is thus most effectually dilated. As the pain increases, the presenting part descends and presses upon the os uteri.

Old nurses often imagine that the pains of the first stage, which they call "niggling" pains, are doing no good, and will accordingly direct their patients to hold their breath and to bear down with all their might. This proceeding is not only useless, but injurious, as such exertions of the voluntary muscles are premature, and only tend to produce exhaustion.

If the hand be placed upon the abdomen during a pain, the whole uterus will be felt to become very firm and hard under contraction.

In primiparæ, the circle formed by the os uteri during dilatation feels much thinner, sharper, and more even than in multiparæ, in whom it is often irregular, and thickened from the effects of previous labours.

Sometimes the child's head, covered by the anterior lip of the os uteri, presses down low into the pelvis even before the commencement of labour; and in such a case, a beginner mistaking it for the bare head, may erroneously conclude that the labour is far advanced in the second stage. A careful vaginal examination will prevent any one from falling into this mistake, for, even if the undilated os uteri is not detected, it will be found that the finger cannot be passed between the presenting body and the pelvis beyond a certain distance, viz., the angle formed by the junction of the vagina and the uterus; whereas, in the second stage of labour, the finger may be passed as high between the head and pelvis as it will reach.

Diagnosis of Presentation.

13. iv. The presentation should always be made out, if possible, before the membranes are ruptured. The ordinary and natural presentation is that of the

crown of the head, or vertex. This is recognized by being larger, rounder, and harder than any other, but,

FIG. 2.

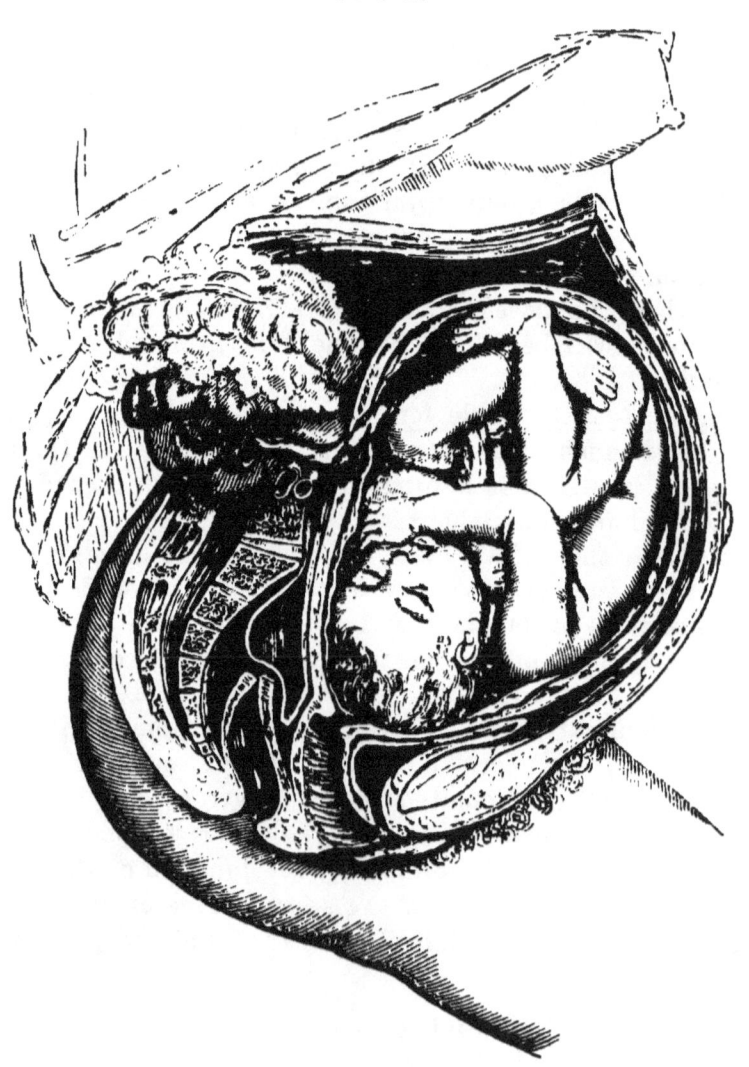

above all, by the divisions or sutures, and spaces or fontanelles between the cranial bones. (*Fig. 2.*)

If the presentation be not recognized until after the membranes are ruptured, the most favourable opportunity for turning or otherwise rectifying malpositions is lost.

In multiparæ the head is usually much higher during the first stage than in primiparæ; and it occasionally lies so much in front and above the pubis, that there is considerable difficulty in reaching it before the membranes are ruptured.

When the sutures and fontanelles can be distinctly felt, it amounts to positive proof of head presentation; as no such structure exists in any other part of the body.

When a Patient can be left.

14. v. A patient in the first stage of labour can be safely left for a short time, under the following circumstances :—*a.* In the case of a primipara, if the presentation be natural, and the os uteri not yet dilated to the size of a crown-piece. *b.* In the case of a multipara, if the pains be few and weak, the presentation natural, and the os uteri not yet dilated to the size of a shilling. *c.* In any case, if there have been very few pains before your arrival, and none for at least an hour afterwards.

a and *b.* Dr. Gooch gives the following judicious advice:—"The propriety of absenting yourself from a patient who is in labour will depend upon many circumstances, but principally upon whether or not it is a first labour. If it is a first labour, provided you can be within call, you may visit your other patients, return, ascertain the state of the labour, and perhaps go out again, &c. This you may do until the os uteri is dilated to the size of a crown-piece; a process which will occupy about two-thirds of the time of labour: afterwards no prudent man would leave his patient until the labour is over. But if it is not the first child, the progress of the labour is very different; the patient has slight pains, occurring about every ten or fifteen minutes, just sufficient to remind her that she is in labour; the accoucheur is generally apprised of this state of things in order that he may be in the way. On being sent for, after a notice of this kind, you will find that these trifling pains have been sufficient, perhaps, completely to dilate the os uteri. The pains now become stronger, and the membranes more distended — presently they are ruptured —gush goes the liquor amnii; and if your arrival has not been pretty expeditious, you may be greeted on entering the room with the squalling of the child under the bed-clothes. If I am called to a labour which is not the first, and find the pains regular though slight, however trifling may be the dilatation of the os uteri, I am exceedingly shy of leaving my patient."

c. If the pains have ceased in consequence of the patient's nervousness at your sudden appearance, you will, by waiting an hour, have allowed ample time for the effects of this feeling to wear off.

Prognosis.

15. After the examination has been made, the patient will probably ask whether all is right? and how long will it be before the labour is over? The first of these questions may be answered in the affirmative, if the head presents and the passages are in proper condition (see 10); but to the second you can only reply that it is impossible to tell with certainty, because the duration of the labour will depend upon the strength and frequency of the pains, and other circumstances which are beyond calculation.

Any attempt to foretell the exact duration, especially of a first labour, would be very likely to end in the exposure of the false prophet, and in the disappointment of the patient.

Progress.

16. When the presentation has been made out, the progress of the labour is to be ascertained by subsequent examinations; but the fewer that are made for this purpose, during the first stage, the better.

Frequent examinations during the first stage cause much discomfort, and tend to render the parts dry and irritable.

It is difficult to lay down any precise rule as to the frequency of examinations; they should in general be made more frequently when the labour is rapid than when it is slow, but never, perhaps, oftener than once in half an hour during the first stage.

Position during First Stage.

17. It is not necessary, during the first stage, to keep the patient on the bed. On the contrary, the pains will be more effectual when she is in the erect posture, either sitting, standing, or walking.

The question of position at this time is one which may safely be left to the patient, who may be allowed to consult her own ease and convenience.

If, however, the pains become feeble upon lying down, she should be encouraged to get up occasionally and walk about the room.

Propriety of Occasional Absence from the Room.

18. The pressure upon the bladder and rectum during labour is apt to cause frequent desire to pass water and to go to stool; you should therefore retire when you can into another room, and thus relieve your patient from the restraint occasioned by your constant presence.

It often happens that amongst the poorest class there is no second room into which the accoucheur can retire; but when, unfortunately, such is the case, the force of habit has probably done much to blunt any feelings of modesty.

Diet during Labour.

19. During the active progress of labour the patient's diet should be very simple. In an ordinary case some tea or gruel, with or without some toast or bread, will be sufficient.

The process of labour interferes with that of digestion, and therefore a full meal is to be avoided.

Signs of Second Stage.

20. The second stage of labour commences with the full dilatation of the os uteri, and terminates with the birth of the child. It is occupied in the expulsion of the child, a process which is effected by the contractions of the uterus, aided by the voluntary muscles, especially those of the abdominal parietes and the diaphragm. The pains are of a peculiar, forcing character, and cause the woman to hold her breath, to fix her limbs, and to bear down with all her might. The low complaints of the first stage commonly give place to a loud outcry before and after each pain.

Position during Second Stage.

21. During the second stage the patient should be kept upon the bed, lying upon her left side. The part of the bed upon which she rests should previously be

"guarded," as it is termed, by covering it with a piece of oil-cloth, sheet india-rubber, or gutta percha, so as to protect it from the discharges, &c. Amongst the poorer classes it is customary to turn up the lower half

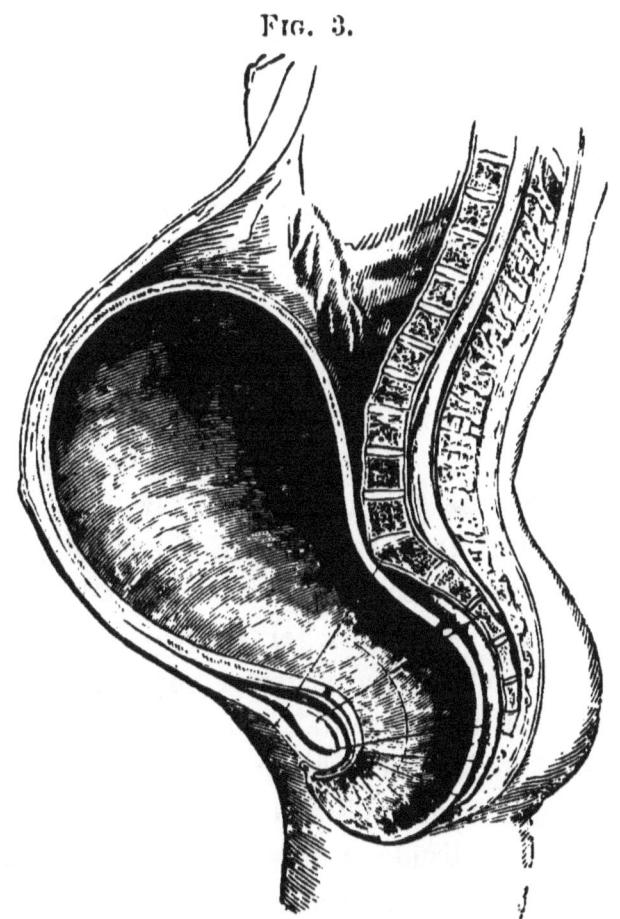

Fig. 3.

Fig. 3 (taken from Dr. Tyler Smith's Manual) represents the uterus and parturient canal in a state of full dilatation.

of the bed, so as to uncover the sacking, upon which a folded sheet, blanket, or piece of carpet, is then placed.

State of Uterus, Vagina, &c., during Second Stage.

22. Vaginal examinations may be made more frequently during the second stage than previously. The os uteri is now fully dilated, so that the uterus and vagina form one continuous canal. (*Fig.* 3.) At this period the membranes are usually ruptured, and the waters escape with a gush.

Vaginal examinations occasion much less annoyance and irritation during the second stage, because the soft parts are well relaxed, and bathed freely, both by liquor amnii and a copious mucous secretion.

The quantity of liquor amnii is very variable; sometimes it is so little that its escape is scarcely apparent; at other times it is sufficiently great to deluge the bed and to pour down on the floor.

Diagnosis of Presentation.

23. As soon as the membranes are ruptured, the exact position of the head should, if possible, be ascertained. The hairy scalp will now be felt distinctly, either loose and wrinkled, or puffy and œdematous; in an ordinary case the posterior superior part of the right parietal bone presents; the occiput of the child is towards the left acetabulum of the mother; the sagittal suture runs obliquely backwards, and from left to right, and divides the vertex unequally into two parts, of which the anterior is the largest and lowest; it commences in front with the triangular space of the posterior fontanelle, and terminates behind with the quadrangular anterior fontanelle, which is opposite the right sacro-iliac synchondrosis, and so high as to be almost out of reach. (*Fig.* 4.)

The state of the scalp will much depend upon the amount of pressure to which the head is subjected. If the labour be quick and easy, the scalp will be likely to be loose and wrinkled; if

Fig. 4.

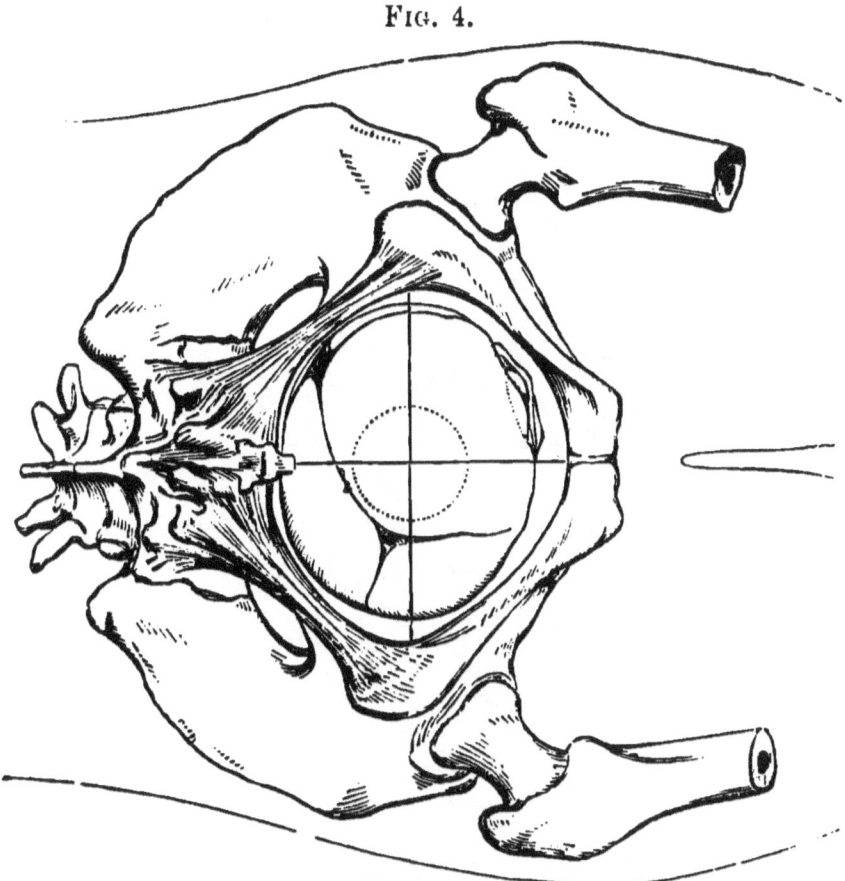

it be slow and difficult, especially if it be a first labour, the presenting part will become tense and œdematous, forming what is called the "caput succedaneum."

Descent of the Head.

24. As the second stage advances, the child's head is felt to press down more and more into the cavity of the pelvis with each pain, and to recede somewhat

18 MANAGEMENT OF ORDINARY LABOUR.

afterwards. Still, each pain gains upon the advance made by its predecessor, and the head gradually fills the hollow of the sacrum, until at last it occupies the outlet of the pelvis, and presses on the perineum. (*Fig. 5.*)

FIG. 5.

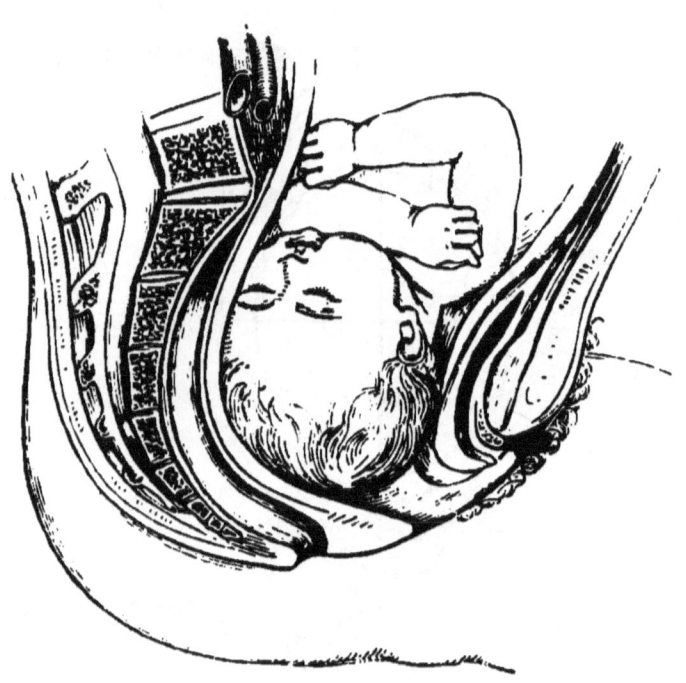

Management during the Pains.

25. During the pains of the second stage, the woman should be encouraged to second the uterine efforts by her own exertions; you may, therefore, direct her to hold her breath, to grasp a towel, which is usually fastened round one of the bedposts for that purpose, and at the same time to press firmly with her feet against the nearest bedpost or the footboard.

MANAGEMENT OF ORDINARY LABOUR. 19

When the extremities are thus fixed, the muscles of the thorax and abdomen will act more advantageously.

Nurses are in the habit of making firm pressure upon the lower part of the woman's back during each pain, and much relief is often thus afforded.

Passage of Head through Outlet.

26. As the head is passing through the outlet of the

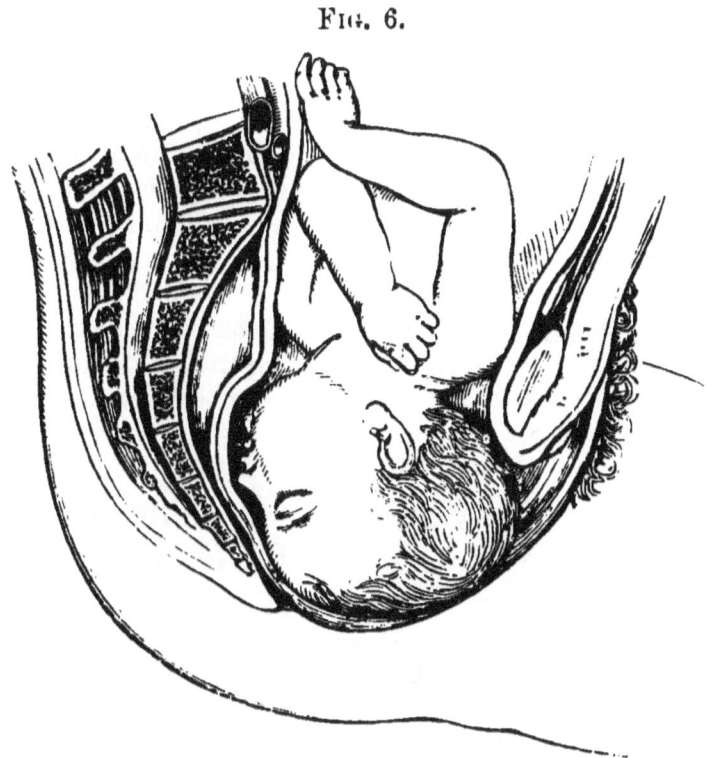

Fig. 6.

pelvis, it loses its former oblique position, and makes a slight turn, so as to bring the occiput beneath the arch of the pubis, and the face opposite the sacrum. At the same time, whilst the occiput is comparatively fixed, the chin becomes separated from the sternum;

the face descending and describing a curve in conformity with the hollow of the sacrum. The perineum, now greatly distended, and much reduced in thickness, covers the head very closely; the anus is also dilated, and its mucous membrane more or less protruded. (*Fig.* 6.)

By the turn just mentioned, which is called the movement of Rotation, the antero-posterior, or long diameters, of the head and pelvic outlet are brought into correspondence.

By the second movement, which is termed Extension, the axis of the head, or occipito-mental diameter, assumes the same direction as the axis of the outlet of the pelvis.

Any fæces which may be contained in the lower part of the rectum are mechanically expelled by the pressure of the head. This is one of the many inconveniences which may result from a loaded state of the rectum.

In first labours, when the perineum is much distended, it is a good plan to expose the part to view, so as to see exactly what is taking place. By skilfully arranging the light and the bedclothes, this may be done without any apparent exposure.

Support of Perineum.

27. It is generally advised that the distended perineum should be supported. This is usually effected by laying the palm of one hand (previously covered by a napkin) flat upon the perineum, with the wrist towards the coccyx and the tips of the fingers forwards, and making pressure upon the part in such a manner as to give the head a proper direction forwards, beneath the pubic arch.*

---

* The author, being convinced of its inutility, has for many years abandoned the practice of supporting the perineum in ordinary cases. He would, however, advise the student, before

The left hand is usually preferred for the support of the perineum, because the right is then free for any other manipulations which may be required.

Expulsion of Head.

28. After a variable time, the resistance of the perineum is overcome, and the head, propelled by two or three long and severe pains, escapes from the vulva. As soon as it is expelled, it resumes its former oblique position, so that the face looks upwards and backwards towards the right hip of the mother.

The dilatation of the perineum, which in multiparæ may be effected in two or three pains, may occasionally in primiparæ occupy a period of several hours. Young accoucheurs should therefore be cautious not to promise a speedy termination under such circumstances.

The vertex and back of the head escape first, whilst the border of the perineum glides successively over the anterior fontanelle, the forehead, and face.

The movement of rotation, which is again performed by the head after its expulsion, is termed Restitution, or External Rotation.

During the latter part of the second stage, the accoucheur should remain sitting at the bedside, making frequent examinations, and noting carefully the exact course and progress of the head.

Interval after Birth of Head.

29. In most cases a short interval elapses after the

---

doing the same, to give the practice a fair trial in a certain number of cases, so as to be able to form his own conclusions respecting its utility. Those who wish to see a full and clear statement of all the reasons that may be adduced against the practice of supporting the perineum will do well to consult a little work on this subject by Dr. Graily Hewitt.

birth of the head before the uterus resumes its action. During this time the child, if vigorous, may breathe, or even cry; but more frequently it is unable to do either, until the body is born and the chest set at liberty.

When the labour is rapid and the pains very powerful, the head and body are not unfrequently expelled by the same pain.

30. Whilst waiting for the expulsion of the body you may support the head of the child with your hand, and remove with your fingers any mucus or portions of membrane which may clog the mouth or fauces. You may also see that everything is ready for the child, and especially that a pair of scissors and a skein or two of stout thread are at hand for the purpose of tying and dividing the cord.

The accoucheur should wait patiently for the uterine contractions, and not attempt to hasten the delivery by pulling at the child's neck and shoulders,—a practice much in favour with old nurses, but very mischievous, because it is likely to leave the uterus uncontracted, and thus to occasion hæmorrhage. (For exception to this rule, see 51, Part II.)

Expulsion of Body.

31. After the birth of the head, the uterus speedily renews its efforts, and expels the rest of the body. Whilst the shoulders are clearing the pelvic outlet, a movement of rotation, similar to that performed by the head, causes the right shoulder to pass beneath the pubic arch, and the left in front of the perineum.

When to separate the Child.

32. A strong, healthy child, as soon as it is born, will begin to breathe freely, and in most cases to cry vigorously. When it has thus given satisfactory proof of its respiratory power, you may at once proceed to separate it from its mother by tying and dividing the umbilical cord.

Ligature and Division of Cord.

33. Having uncovered the child, so as to see what you are about, place a ligature, consisting of three or four pieces of stout thread, around the cord, about three fingers' breadth from the navel, and tie it tightly with a firm double knot; then place another similar ligature about an inch farther from the navel, and divide the cord between the two with a pair of scissors. You then give the child to the nurse, who wraps it up in a piece of flannel called a " receiver," and carries it off to the fireside to be washed and dressed.

As soon as the child is born, the accoucheur should see that the air has free access to its face, and that its mouth and nose are not covered by bed-clothes, &c.

In uncovering the child, the clothes should be tucked in round the mother, so as to avoid any exposure of her person.

If the accoucheur divide the cord carelessly beneath the bed-clothes, without seeing what he is about, he may amputate, at the same time, portions of the child's fingers, toes, or even penis, as in cases related by Denman, Merriman, and others.

The threads of which the ligatures consist should, before being used, be united together by a knot at each end. The ligature nearest to the umbilicus is necessary to prevent the child from bleeding to death by hæmorrhage from the divided umbilical vessels. The other ligature is not absolutely necessary, but is used chiefly for the sake of cleanliness, to prevent the blood contained in the rest of the cord from spurting out upon the bed or the clothes of the accoucheur.

Before the child is given to the nurse, the portion of cord attached to it should be examined, to ascertain that the ligature remains firm, and that there is no oozing of blood from the umbilical vessels.

As soon as the child is born, the mother may be informed as to its sex; and, if the child be healthy and well formed, she may be satisfied upon these points also; but if there be any defect or malformation, she should not be told of it too soon or abruptly.

Third Stage of Labour.

34. The third stage of labour is occupied in the expulsion of the after-birth. The birth of the child is generally followed by a short interval of repose, after which three or four pains set in, which are frequently accompanied with some discharge of blood, and resemble those of the first stage in character. By means of these contractions the uterus casts off the after-birth, sometimes completely beyond the vulva, but more often into the upper part of the vagina.

The period of repose immediately following the birth of the child is generally free from pain, and is a delightful contrast to the preceding suffering.

It occasionally happens, when uterine action is very energetic, that the child and placenta are expelled together by the same pain. From the flow of blood which accompanies them, the pains of the third stage have been called the "dolores cruenti." The blood escapes from the venous orifices which have been laid open by the separation of the placenta from the inner surface of the uterus. In some cases, however, there is apparently no escape whatever. The quantity of blood which escapes with the placenta is very variable ;* it may be as little as a table-spoonful, or as much as a pint without producing any material effect on the patient: if it exceeds the latter quantity, it will be likely to produce a marked constitutional effect, as indicated by the pulse, &c. ; the case then becomes one of post-partum hæmorrhage, and is to be treated accordingly. (See 57, Part II.)

Necessity of making Abdominal Examination in Third Stage.

35. As soon as you have given the child to the nurse, you should make it an invariable rule to place your hand upon the patient's abdomen, for the purpose of examining the uterus. In most cases it will be distinctly felt reaching as high as the umbilicus, and becoming perceptibly harder, so that its limits can be easily defined. When it is in this state, it is beginning to contract, but has not yet expelled the placenta. On making an ordinary vaginal examination, you can feel the cord only, but no portion of the placenta.

By means of an abdominal examination, you can satisfy yourself, from the greatly reduced bulk of the uterus, not only that that organ is contracting upon the placenta, but that it does not contain a second child. (See 40, Part II.)

With respect to the management of the third stage of labour, Dr. Spiegelberg has well remarked :—" A constant supervision of the uterus from the moment the head is delivered, by which general contraction of the uterus and detachment of the placenta are insured, is the main point."

Duration of Third Stage.

36. The average duration of the third stage, reckon-

---

* Dr. Champneys considers that it amounts, on an average, to twelve ounces (*Obstetrical Transactions* for 1887, p. 166).

ing from the birth of the child to the expulsion of the after-birth, is about a quarter of an hour. During this time you should sit by the bedside occasionally examining the abdomen, and waiting patiently until the placenta is detached by the natural efforts; but you should on no account attempt to hasten that process by pulling at the funis.

The time occupied by the third stage is exceedingly variable; sometimes the placenta follows immediately, or in five minutes after the birth of the child; at other times it is not expelled until twenty minutes, half an hour, or even more, have elapsed. When it remains more than an hour in the uterus, the case may be considered as one of retained placenta, and treated accordingly. (See 36, Part III.)

Traction of the cord when the placenta is still attached, and especially where the uterus is uncontracted, may produce the most disastrous consequences. It may cause—1. Copious hæmorrhage from partial detachment of the placenta. 2. Inversion of the uterus. 3. Separation of the cord from the placenta. 4. Irregular or hour-glass contraction of the uterus.

How to aid Expulsion of Placenta.

37. If the placenta should not be expelled in a quarter of an hour, you may aid the uterine efforts by external pressure. For this purpose, grasp the fundus uteri in the hollow of the hand, and as soon as it is felt to harden, make strong and firm pressure upon it, downwards and backwards, in the axis of the pelvic brim.

This mode of promoting expulsion has been called "Expression of the placenta." Although long known to many accoucheurs in this country, especially in Dublin, it has not been made of so much account as in Germany, where it has been dignified by the name of "Credè's method," from the writer who has chiefly recommended it.

Dr. McClintock has pointed out that it is not a good plan to attempt to remove the placenta before a quarter of an hour has elapsed; because sufficient time has not been allowed for the blood to coagulate in the uterine sinuses.

In most cases, where the expulsion of the placenta has been aided by pressure as above described, no further manipulations will be required for its removal.

How to ascertain if Placenta is Detached.

38. In many cases, the placenta, after being detached and expelled from the uterine cavity, is found resting on the os tincæ, or in the upper part of the vagina. You know that it is in this situation, and may at once proceed to remove it, if, in making an ordinary vaginal examination, you can feel with your finger not only the insertion of the cord, but also a considerable portion of the body of the placenta.

If these cases are left to nature, the placenta may remain several hours before the vagina has regained sufficient contractility to expel it.

In general, it is enough to be able to feel the insertion of the cord in order to be assured that the placenta is detached, but it is not always so; because in what are called "battledore" placentæ, the cord may be inserted into the lower edge of the placenta, and this portion may be readily reached, although the chief part of the organ is still attached to the uterus.

How to remove a Detached Placenta.

39. To remove the placenta from the vagina, hold the cord firmly in the right hand, and grasp the lowest or presenting edge between the fore and middle fingers and the thumb of the left hand, and then make steady

traction, first in the direction of the inlet, and afterwards of the outlet, of the pelvis.

When the placenta is expelled naturally, Dr. Matthews Duncan states that it is folded inwards upon itself, so that some portion of its circumference first descends and becomes the presenting part. On the other hand, some very careful investigations that have been recently made by Dr. Champneys tend to confirm the views of Schultze, and to show that no part of the edge of the placenta usually presents, but a point on its amniotic surface within two inches of its lower edge. However this may be, to remove the placenta in the way usually recommended, viz., by simply pulling at the cord, is not in accordance with the natural process, because the placenta is thus inverted, so that the central portion becomes the presenting part. In this way it is made to act as a sucker, whilst its entire circumference is brought down simultaneously, so as to add considerably to the difficulty of extraction.

To prevent the cord from slipping, it should be grasped with a napkin, or a coil of it twisted round the fingers of the right hand. By means of the fingers of the left hand, you can readily feel if the cord is beginning to give way near its insertion. Should this be the case, you must at once desist from further traction upon it, and endeavour instead to draw down the placenta solely by the fingers of the left hand, or, if necessary, introduce the entire hand to remove it.

How to remove Membranes.

40. In all cases, as soon as the placenta is beyond the os externum, it should be turned round and round several times before being taken away. By this means the membranes, trailing behind it, are twisted into a rope, in which form they are much less likely to be torn, and are more readily withdrawn from the vagina.

"The placenta when delivered must be carefully examined, so as to make sure that everything belonging to it has actually come away" (*Spiegelberg's Midwifery*, p. 264).

Any portions of membranes or clots, which may remain behind after the placenta, are to be also taken away.

The placenta, when removed, is to be put into a chamber utensil, which should be at hand to receive it. It is afterwards taken away by the nurse and burnt, in accordance with a popular custom of long standing.

State of Uterus after Expulsion of Placenta.

41. As soon as the placenta has come away, you should again make an abdominal examination. For this purpose it is better to place the woman on her back with her legs extended. If the uterus be properly contracted, you will feel it through the parietes, somewhere between the umbilicus and pubis, as a hard round mass, about the size and firmness of a child's head at birth.

Nature guards against hæmorrhage from the open venous sinuses by contraction of the uterine fibres. By this means each bleeding vessel is secured as effectually as by a ligature. No medical man should feel satisfied in leaving his patient until the uterus has contracted properly.

The uterus is seldom found to be quite in the middle line, but is more often inclined to one side, especially to the right.

Rigors after Labour—their Treatment.

42. The heat and perspiration produced by the violent exertions of the second stage are likely to be followed by chilliness, when the labour is over. You may, therefore, remove the soiled sheet from beneath the patient, and substitute a warm, dry napkin, and also apply to the external genitals a similar napkin,

which the nurse usually keeps in readiness for the purpose. You may likewise direct the nurse to throw an extra blanket over her, and to give her some warm drink, such as tea or gruel.

Nurses are very fond of adding some spirits to the tea or gruel; but, as a general rule, such stimulants should be forbidden, unless the patient appear exhausted, when it will be a good plan to give an egg beaten up with a table-spoonful of brandy. As the ordinary manipulations of labour are now concluded, the medical attendant is at liberty to leave the bedside for a short time to wash his hands, &c., but he should not be long away from his patient.

How to wrap up the Cord.

43. Whilst the nurse is dressing the child, you may examine the remnant of cord attached to the abdomen. For the sake of cleanliness it is usually passed through a hole in the centre of a square piece of soft linen rag, in which it is enveloped, and then turned up on the abdomen. To keep it in place, a broad piece of flannel is passed round the child's body and secured by stitches. The portion of cord withers, and generally drops off about the end of a week.

Nurses have a prejudice in favour of *scorched* rag, which they use under the idea that it promotes in some manner the cicatrization of the umbilicus after the separation of the cord.

Abdominal Bandage.

44. A broad bandage should be applied round the abdomen, in order to support that part, and maintain uterine contraction. The bandage should consist of a piece of strong jean or calico about four feet long, and

fourteen or sixteen inches wide. It should be drawn firmly round the abdomen, so as to cover it completely, from the ensiform cartilage to the pubis, and should be low enough to embrace the femoral trochanters, otherwise it will be likely to slip upwards. The ends of the bandage should then be secured by five or six strong pins.

The abdominal bandage is not unfrequently applied by the nurse, or other female attendant ; but in all cases, when there is any doubt as to the proper contraction of the uterus, it is far better that the medical attendant should put on the bandage himself. In cases of this kind it should be put on much earlier ; and sometimes it is proper to do so even before the birth of the child. The abdominal bandage should be continued for at least a fortnight.

Necessity of Repose after Labour.

45. The woman should be allowed to lie quiet for at least an hour after the birth of the child. At the end of this time the attendants may change her dress, and place her comfortably in bed ; taking care, whilst so doing, not to raise her in the least from the recumbent posture.

Amongst the poor, women are usually confined in their ordinary clothes ; they have therefore to undergo the whole process of undressing afterwards. Whilst this is done, they ought to remain passive in the hands of their attendants, and should on no account be allowed to undress themselves.

When the Patient may be left.

46. You should not leave the patient's house for at least an hour after the termination of the labour. During this time you may occasionally look at her,

feel her pulse, examine her abdomen, &c. Before leaving, you should always make a point of examining the condition of the uterus, to ascertain whether it *remains* properly contracted.

The pulse, which during the second stage was much elevated, soon after labour subsides to, or even falls below, the ordinary standard. Hence, an unnaturally quick pulse half an hour or an hour after delivery is often an unfavourable symptom, and not unfrequently forebodes hæmorrhage. (See note 55, Part II.)

Sometimes the uterus, after contracting, again relaxes, and hæmorrhage is the result. The accoucheur should therefore satisfy himself, not only that the uterus is in a state of contraction, but that this condition is likely to be permanent.

An elevation of temperature is commonly observed within the first six hours after delivery, and need occasion no alarm if it does not exceed 102°, and is accompanied with but slight acceleration of pulse. According to Schroeder, the elevation of temperature is caused by the gradually increased production of heat through rapid metamorphosis of the uterus. After about twenty hours, the temperature falls to the ordinary standard.

Necessity of Rest after Delivery.

47. The lying-in chamber should be kept perfectly quiet, so as to allow the patient to sleep, or at all events to repose for some hours after her fatigues. When she has thus rested, the infant may be put to the breast; and this ought to be done within twelve hours after delivery.

The room should be darkened for a time by drawing down the blinds, and to ensure tranquillity as few persons as possible should be admitted into it. The visits of gossiping friends and neighbours should be strictly prohibited. The room should also be well ventilated and not too warm as is often the case amongst the poor, who will light up a large fire, in a small close room, in the middle of summer.

The late Dr. Rigby used to recommend that the child should be applied to the breast immediately after delivery; in some cases, especially when there is a tendency to hæmorrhage, this may be advisable; but in general it is better to allow the woman to rest for some time previously. However, it is always far preferable to apply the child to the breast too soon than too late.

How often the Patient is to be visited.

48. The frequency of your visits after a labour must be regulated very much by circumstances. As a general rule, you should see your patient twice within the first twenty-four hours, and once every day during the first week; then every second, third, or fourth day during the following week; after which, if all goes on well, you may take your leave.

Inquiries to be made at First Visit.

49. Your first visit should be within twelve hours after delivery. After feeling your patient's pulse and looking at her tongue, you may ask if she has had any sleep, and has been free from pain; if there is any sign of milk; if there is a plentiful "discharge," and if she has passed water, or had any action of the bowels. Respecting the child, you may ask if it has cried or slept; if it has been put to the breast; and if it has passed water or stools.

Women very frequently cannot sleep, for some hours afte delivery, in consequence of the occurrence of after-pains these, after some hours, subside of themselves, and as a genera rule, require no treatment. (See 61, Part II.)

The first evacuations from the child's bowels consist of a substance called meconium, which is of a dark greenish-brown colour, somewhat resembling treacle in appearance and consistence. If there be any doubt as to the child's ability to pass urine or fæces, an examination should be made to ascertain that there is no malformation, such as imperforate anus, urethra, &c.

Secretion of Milk.

50. The secretion of milk commences within twelve hours after delivery, but is seldom fully established before the end of the third day. As the secretion becomes plentiful, the breasts harden and enlarge, their swelling occasioning feelings of tension, and sometimes even sharp darting pains. The first milk is called colostrum; it is of a yellowish colour, and has a purgative effect upon the child.

The colostrum is the natural purgative of a newly-born infant. If a child be put to the breast sufficiently early, it will require none of the castor-oil, sugar and butter, &c., which nurses are so fond of giving for this purpose.

Newly-born children seldom require any food in addition to the breast. Should, however, the secretion of milk be scanty, or tardy in making its appearance, it may be necessary to give the child some food.

The best ordinary substitute for the mother's milk is a mixture of equal parts of cow's milk and water sweetened with a little sugar. The child should suck this from a proper feeding-bottle. The condensed Swiss milk will often answer better than cow's milk, especially if of indifferent quality. It should be given in the proportion of a tea-spoonful to a quarter of a pint of water.

It is not well, however, to continue it after the first three or four months.

Excretion of Urine and Fæces.

51. After an ordinary labour there is seldom any

difficulty in passing water, but the bowels rarely act without medicine; on this account, if they have not been previously moved, it is a general rule to give a dose of castor-oil on the morning of the third day; one table-spoonful is mostly sufficient, which may be repeated after six hours, if necessary.

It is a good plan to direct that the woman should pass water whilst leaning forward in bed upon her elbows and knees; because this position readily allows the escape of any retained clots, portions of membranes, &c.

Lochial Discharge.

52. The secretion of the uterus after delivery is called the lochia, or in common language, "the cleansings." It at first bears much resemblance to ordinary menstrual discharge, being plentiful, of a red colour, and peculiar odour, and frequently containing clots, shreds of membrane, &c. In a few days it becomes less abundant, and paler in colour, changing to brown, yellow, or green (when it is sometimes termed the "green waters"), until at last it is clear and transparent; it usually ceases by the end of the third week.

During the first week or two after delivery, the whole of the decidual lining of the uterus softens, breaks up, and is discharged with the lochia.

Diet after Delivery.

53. The diet of a woman for the first three days after delivery should be chiefly farinaceous: you may allow bread, milk, tea, gruel, arrowroot, sago, &c., with the addition in some cases of broth or beef-tea.

On the fourth day some solid animal food may be given. At the end of a week, if all goes on well, the woman may resume her ordinary diet, and take in addition a little wine, beer, or porter, if required.

A light, unstimulating diet is proper, until the secretion of milk is fully established, and until any feverishness, which may accompany this process, has quite subsided. As the process of lactation subsequently makes a great demand on the powers of the system, a generous diet becomes necessary.

Exercise and General Management.

54. During the first week after delivery, the woman should remain in bed, and be kept strictly in the recumbent position. During the second week, she may put on a loose dress, and lie on a sofa, or recline in an easy chair, taking care to stand or sit upright as little as possible. During the third week, she may sit up, leave her room, and walk a little about the house. If the weather be warm and favourable, she may go out of doors after the end of the third week; but in winter it is better to wait until the end of the month, at least.

It is a common and a good rule amongst nurses that the patient should not be allowed to get up until after the ninth day.

Displacements, such as prolapsus uteri, are very likely to be caused by getting up too soon after delivery; the frequency of such complaints among the poor is thus accounted for. Secondary hæmorrhage, also, may be thus produced.

The process of "involution," *i.e.*, the restoration of the womb to its previous unimpregnated condition, is seldom completed before the end of two months. Any undue exertion is therefore to be avoided before that time.

PART II.

CASES WHICH THE STUDENT MAY UNDERTAKE WITHOUT ASSISTANCE.

Cases of supposed Pregnancy.

1. A WOMAN sends for you who believes herself to be in labour, but who in reality is not pregnant. You may know that such is the case, and may at once undeceive her, if, on making a vaginal examination, you find that there is no shortening of the neck, and no enlargement of the body, of the uterus.

The cases which may simulate pregnancy, and even commencing labour, are usually those in which there is suppression of the menses, with enlargement of the abdomen, from tumours or cysts of various kinds, accompanied with a want of tone and a tympanitic distension of the bowels. Such symptoms are most frequently met with in women approaching the " turn of life," or the age at which the menses cease. In these cases the more conclusive signs of pregnancy, such as the sounds of the fœtal heart and ballottement, are, of course, wanting.

In the unimpregnated state the cervix uteri forms a conical projection, about three-quarters of an inch or an inch long, into the upper part of the vagina.

The absence of shortening in the uterine neck denotes either the absence of pregnancy, or, at all events, the non-completion of the first half of utero-gestation.

The absence of any enlargement of the body of the uterus denotes the absence of pregnancy. To ascertain this, the uterus should be poised on the forefinger of one hand, whilst the other hand is pressed on the hypogastrium. By pressing on its neck, either behind or in front, the uterus may be made to swing backwards and forwards, and thus its weight and mobility may be estimated. By passing the finger as high as possible round the uterine neck, any bulging or increased size of the body may be recognized.

Abortion—Diagnosis.

2. A woman in the first four or five months of her pregnancy sends for you, because she has experienced periodical pains, like those of the first stage of labour. In all probability, abortion is imminent; but you may feel sure of this, if the pains are followed by hæmorrhage from the vagina, and especially if you find that they cause the os uteri to dilate, and the ovum to protrude through it.

By the term abortion is implied the expulsion of the fœtus before the period of its legal viability, which has been fixed at seven lunar months. Abortion is much more frequent during the first two months than at a more advanced period of pregnancy.

Vaginal examinations, in these cases, should be made with much gentleness and care, lest the tendency to abortion should be thereby increased.

Treatment of Abortion.

3. If the pains are few, the hæmorrhage little or none, and the os uteri not open enough to admit the

finger, you may hope to prevent miscarriage. Accordingly you enjoin perfect rest in the horizontal posture, in a cool room. You then endeavour to check uterine action by opiates. For instance, you may give a draught containing ♏xx. of liq. opii sedat. immediately, to be repeated in an hour, and then followed every two hours by a mixture containing ♏v. of liq. opii sedat. and ʒj. of infus. rosæ acid. to each dose; or you may give an enema of ♏xx. of laudanum in ʒiss. of gruel every hour until the pains are checked.

When the patient is plethoric, general or local bleeding may be required in conjunction with opiates; but before resorting to this measure, the student had better send for further advice.

Treatment of Abortion—Premature Labour.

4. If, however, the pains are frequent and increasing in severity, and especially if you can feel the ovum protruding, there is but little hope of checking the miscarriage; the case may then be left to nature. But as various accidents (see Part III., 1 and 2) may occur during and after miscarriage, it requires quite as much watching as a labour at the full term.

The clots which come away in the course of an abortion should be carefully inspected, to see if they contain the entire ovum, or any portions of it, such as membranes, &c.

Miscarriages are called premature labours when they take place during the viability of the fœtus; that is, after the seventh month. They differ from abortions in being accompanied by little or no hæmorrhage, and bear more resemblance to labours at the full term. The means recommended for the arrest of abortion are to be employed with a view to prevent premature delivery

Spurious Pains—Diagnosis.

5. Women, towards the end of pregnancy, occasionally suffer from spurious pains which simulate those of labour. They are distinguished from true labour-pains by their partial and irregular character; but principally by their being unaccompanied with "show," and causing no dilatation of the os uteri.

False pains are mostly limited to the fundus uteri, and are felt in the abdomen chiefly, around the umbilicus; whilst true pains are felt mostly in the back and thighs, and affect the whole uterus, but especially the os tincæ.

Spurious Pains—Treatment.

6. Spurious pains may arise from colic caused by constipation, errors of diet, &c., or from rheumatism of the uterus, in consequence of cold. Their treatment should depend very much upon their cause. In general they may be checked by aperients, such as a dose of castor-oil, or a warm-water enema followed by sedatives, as ♏xx. of tinct. opii, or gr. x. of Dover's powder.

Spurious pains should always be checked, as they tend to exhaust the woman, and are productive of no good; nay, they may even retard labour, if it has already commenced.

Vomiting during Labour.

7. Vomiting is a very frequent occurrence during labour, particularly towards the end of the first stage. The matter ejected usually consists of mucus, together with any food or drink that has been last taken. It is by no means an unfavourable occurrence, and very rarely requires any treatment.

The vomiting appears to depend on a kind of sympathy between the stomach and the uterus, and is mostly observed at the time when the os uteri is rapidly giving way to the dilating pains. It is a common saying amongst nurses, that "sick labours are safe:" but it is far otherwise when vomiting comes on after a prolonged second stage, and is accompanied with great prostration, &c. (See Part III., 30.)

Retarded Labour from Loaded Rectum.

8. Labour is sometimes retarded by a loaded rectum. In such cases an indurated cylinder is felt at the back of the vagina, which might be mistaken by an inexperienced person for a prominent sacrum. By a careful vaginal examination you may distinguish the scybalous masses, and may partially displace them by pressure. The proper treatment is to empty the rectum by an enema of warm water, or, if this fails, by an enema of a pint of warm gruel containing ʒss. of ol. terebinth., and the same quantity of ol. ricini mixed up with the yolk of an egg.

A loaded state of the rectum is a fertile source of spurious pains, as well as a mechanical obstacle to delivery. The obstacle thus presented is seldom insuperable, for the descending head will at last, after much pain to the patient, and greatly to the annoyance of the practitioner, mechanically expel the contents of the rectum.

Should the above-mentioned enema fail, it will be necessary to break up the hardened mass of fæces with a wooden scoop, or the handle of a spoon, and then to repeat the enema; but as this proceeding requires some care in manipulation, it will be more prudent first to send for further advice.

Tedious First Stage.

9. The first stage of labour is sometimes very

tedious, from various causes, such as inefficient uterine action, rigidity of the soft parts, &c.; especially in primiparæ, and, above all, in those who are not young. In such cases the first stage may last many days. In general, the only remedy is time and patience. The delay, although fatiguing to all parties, is very rarely dangerous; you should, therefore, do all you can to cheer your patient and keep up her spirits.

The medical attendant should frequently leave the patient's room, and above all, should beware of making frequent examinations. He should assure her that her labour has barely commenced, and that there is no danger. Dr. Churchill's statistics abundantly prove how little danger attends a prolonged first stage.

Inefficient Uterine Action—Treatment.

10. Inefficient uterine action may arise from natural delicacy of constitution, or from any debilitating cause, either mental or bodily. If the patient be not a primipara, if she has had good labours previously, if the vertex present, and if, in short, you are sure there is no mechanical obstacle to delivery, you may give ergot of rye to increase uterine action; but you should not venture to do so without a consultation, provided any of these conditions are absent.

The ergot may be given in three doses, at intervals of about a quarter of an hour. The bruised or powdered grains will, if good, answer best. Two drachms of the powder should be mixed with half a pint of boiling water, and allowed to simmer a few minutes over the fire. One-third of this decoction should be given (grounds and all) every quarter of an hour. Or instead of the powder, the Extract. Ergotæ Liquid. may be given in ʒss. doses.

During the progress of a tedious labour, when there is much debility, beef-tea and wine should be given frequently.

Tedious Labour from Want of Sleep—Treatment.

11. Inefficient uterine action not unfrequently arises from want of sleep and restlessness, caused by a prolonged first stage, and thus tends still further to produce delay. In such cases the administration of a sedative is attended with the best results. After a sound sleep, the patient awakes refreshed, and the pains set in with renewed vigour.

Twenty minims of Tinct. Opii or 20 grains of Hydrate of Chloral may be given and repeated after three hours, if necessary. As a hypnotic, Hydrate of Chloral is, in some respects, superior to Opium. It may be conveniently given as follows:—

℞ Syrup. Chloral., B.P., ʒss.
  Aquæ, ʒiiiss.
M., sumat dimidiam part. statim.

Rigid Os Uteri—Treatment.

12. Rigidity of the os uteri is a frequent cause of delay in the first stage of labour. It is most usual in primiparæ, and chiefly in those who have passed the age of thirty-five or forty. The rigid os will generally give way and the labour terminate favourably, provided sufficient time be given. If it does not, Chloral may be given as above (No. 11). The whole may be divided into three doses, one to be taken every twenty minutes.

It was formerly the custom to bleed and give Opium and Tartar Emetic in these cases; but these remedies have been superseded in the present day by Chloroform and Chloral. Still, in some exceptional cases, when the woman is plethoric, a moderate bleeding may occasionally be of advantage. It would be well, however, before resorting to such measures, to request further advice.

Premature Rupture of Membranes.

13. Premature rupture of the membranes may be a cause of a tedious first stage; the os uteri being dilated much more slowly and painfully by the child's head than by the bag of the membranes. This is most likely to happen in first labours. In such cases all that is required is time and patience. If there be unusual difficulty, the remedies for an undilatable os uteri are indicated.

It occasionally happens in such cases that the anterior lip of the os uteri becomes swollen and œdematous from pressure between the head and the os pubis. This state of things will nearly always rectify itself in time ; but if it should not, the anterior lip may, in the interval of a pain, be raised by the finger above the crown of the head, and kept there during two or three pains, until it is fully retracted.

Unusual Toughness of Membranes.

14. Labour is sometimes retarded by unusual toughness of the membranes. Long after the os uteri is fully dilated, the membranes may remain entire, and the pains, in consequence, not put on the forcing character of the second stage. To remedy this, you should rupture the membranes, by pressing firmly upon them with the forefinger, when they are rendered tense by a pain. Should this fail, you may notch the finger-nail like a saw, and rub it to and fro on the bag of the membranes until it gives way.

The membranes should on no account be ruptured, until it is quite certain they have answered their purpose, by completely dilating the os uteri.

Anterior Obliquity of Uterus.

15. In some multiparæ, the abdominal parietes may be so relaxed as to allow the fundus uteri to fall very much forwards. This anterior obliquity of the uterus is called, in common language, "pendulous belly," and may be a cause of tedious labour. The os uteri is thrown so much upwards and backwards towards the sacrum, as to be almost out of reach. The remedy is, to support the belly by means of a broad bandage, and to keep the woman lying on her back during the pains.

In addition to the anterior obliquity just described, the fundus uteri may be inclined to either side, constituting lateral obliquity. This species requires much the same management as the preceding, viz., to support the abdomen, and to place the patient on the opposite side to that towards which the fundus uteri is inclined.

Inhalation of Chloroform during Labour.

16. In midwifery practice chloroform is the anæsthetic usually employed. It should, as a general rule, be used during the second stage only. It is especially indicated in first labours, when there is much rigidity of the soft parts and an unusual amount of suffering.

Chloroform during ordinary labour is a luxury and not a necessity; for in the majority of cases it does not add to the safety of the patient, and there is no doubt that normal labours do quite as well without it. It is expensive, and therefore the poor, whom students have to attend, do not, as a rule, ask for it or expect it. Still, in exceptional cases, such as those mentioned above, it is a great boon both to the patient and practitioner, and should not be withheld on the ground of expense.

During the first stage of labour, Chloral, as recommended above (No. 11), is preferable.

Mode of Administering Chloroform.

17. Chloroform is most conveniently administered upon a folded handkerchief or napkin, which should be held near, but not in contact with, the face. It should be given immediately before each pain, and removed as soon as the pain is over. It may be given with more freedom towards the end of the labour; but it is better just to stop short of producing complete unconsciousness.

The handkerchief or napkin should be folded in a conical form, and wetted with Chloroform by pressing it on the open mouth of the inverted bottle, just as if we wished to scent it with Eau-de-Cologne. There is not time to measure the quantity in a minim glass, just as the pain comes on, nor is it necessary for safety to be so exact.

If, in consequence of a weak action of the patient's heart, there is any doubt as to the safety of administering pure Chloroform, it will be advisable to mix it with any equal quantity of Sulphuric Ether, Spirits of Wine, or Eau-de-Cologne. Should there be any tendency to syncope, or should the breathing become stertorous, it will be as well to at once remove the Chloroform. It should also be removed if it evidently tends to weaken the pains, and should be avoided in the case of multiparæ who are known to be subject to post-partum hæmorrhage. If any anæsthetic be employed in such cases, Ether is preferable.

Undilatable Vagina and Perineum—Treatment.

18. Delay may be occasioned in the second stage of labour by a rigid undilatable condition of the vagina

and perineum. This state is peculiar to primiparæ, especially such as are not young, and in these the dilatation of those parts may occupy several hours. The parts feel dry and tense, and admit the finger with difficulty. To promote their dilatation, you may use warm fomentations and inunctions, or you may direct the woman to sit over a pan of warm water. Should these means fail, the remedies for an undilatable os uteri are indicated. (See Part II., 12.)

Chloroform is sometimes of great use in these cases.

Presentations with Forehead anteriorly—Diagnosis.

19. Labour may be retarded in the second stage by unfavourable presentations of various kinds. Thus, in some presentations of the vertex, the forehead may be in the anterior, instead of in the posterior, semicircle of the pelvis. You may ascertain that the head is in this position, even before the os uteri is fully dilated or the membranes ruptured, by noticing that the posterior lip of the os uteri is much lower in the pelvis than the anterior lip. (*Fig.* 7, 1.) After the rupture of the membranes, the posterior fontanelle will be found in the posterior half of the pelvis, and the anterior fontanelle in the anterior half, behind one or other groin.

The depression of the posterior lip of the os uteri depends on the following circumstances :—In ordinary labour the child's head is at the commencement of the labour flexed upon its body; but during its progress the head becomes still more flexed by the chin approaching still nearer to the sternum. The result of this is, that the posterior half of the child's head is much lower than the anterior. Consequently, in the occipito-anterior presentations, the occiput being in front, presses upon the anterior lip of the os uteri, and depresses it

FIG. 7.

1. *Occipito-posterior Presentation.*

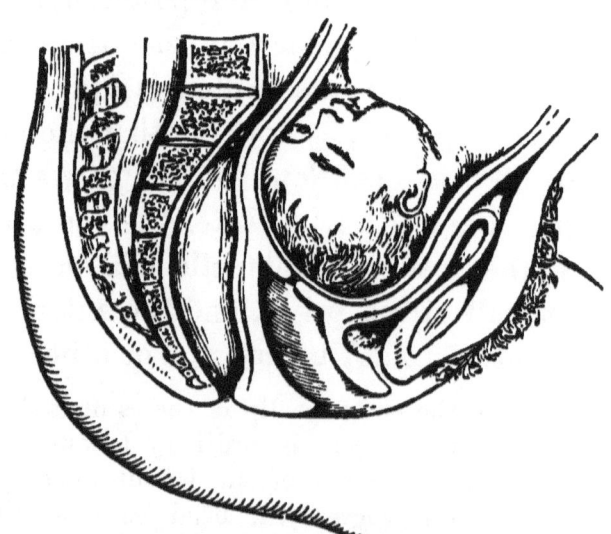

2. *Occipito-anterior Presentation.*

much below the level of the posterior lip. (*Fig.* 7, 2.) But in occipito-posterior presentations the reverse takes place: the occiput being behind, depresses the posterior below the anterior lip. (*Fig.* 7, 1.) Hence the shape and position of the os, on making a vaginal examination, appear to be very different from those which we ordinarily find. In ordinary cases the finger passes but a slight distance into the angle, or cul-de-sac, formed by the junction of the vagina and the anterior lip of the os. (See *Fig.* 2.) But in the occipito-posterior positions the finger passes high up behind the symphysis pubis into the cul-de-sac just mentioned, which in this case forms an acute angle, as in the first it formed an obtuse angle. At the same time the posterior lip, and even the entire os, is unusually low in the pelvis.*

Presentations of Forehead anteriorly—how altered by Nature.

20. Many of these cases will be converted by the natural efforts into ordinary vertex presentation. Thus, as the head descends into the pelvis, it will perform a movement of rotation, the forehead moving backwards from the acetabulum to the sacro-iliac synchondrosis on one side, and the occiput moving forwards in a similar way on the opposite. This movement may be effected artificially, provided the second stage be not too far advanced.

Dr. Ramsbotham thus describes the mode in which such presentations should be altered:—"Presuming that, after a number of tolerably strong expulsive pains, no advance takes place in the situation of the head, it will then be proper to embrace the cranium between the first three fingers and the thumb of one or other hand, and to give the face an inclination

---

* See paper by the author on *Varieties of Cranial Presentation,* "British Medical Journal," Feb. 4th, 1852.

to the right or left ilium, according as its original direction was to the right or left groin ; and this attempt must be made in the absence of uterine contraction, and before the head has become locked in the pelvic cavity: for if it be delayed till a state of impaction has occurred, the malposition cannot be remedied by the power of the hand alone, and instruments will most likely be required in order to finish the delivery."

The student will do well not to take upon himself the responsibility of altering one of these presentations, because such a proceeding requires an amount of tact and skill which can only be acquired by experience.

Labour where Forehead continues in Anterior Semicircle.

21. But in many instances the turn above described does not take place, and the forehead continues in the anterior semicircle. The labour is thus rendered more tedious, but is nevertheless, with but few exceptions, accomplished by the natural efforts. The head, as it presses down into the cavity of the pelvis, becomes more and more flexed on the body, until at last the anterior fontanelle is placed beneath the pubic arch, and the occiput presses on the perineum, causing more distension of that part than usual. Finally, the occiput is expelled first, and then the forehead and face. (*Fig.* 8.)

In ordinary labour, as the head passes through the outlet of the pelvis, the chin leaves the chest, and the head is extended upon the body ; in occipito-anterior presentations the reverse takes place, and hence the long axes of the child's head and body are not so well adapted to the axes of the pelvis; but there is reason to believe that the difficulties of such presentations have been much overrated, upon grounds which are more theoretical than practical. Thus it has been stated that, in consequence of its shape being more square, the forehead does not adapt itself so well as the occiput to the arch of the pubis, as the head clears the outlet of the pelvis; without considering how materially that shape may be altered

Fig. 8.

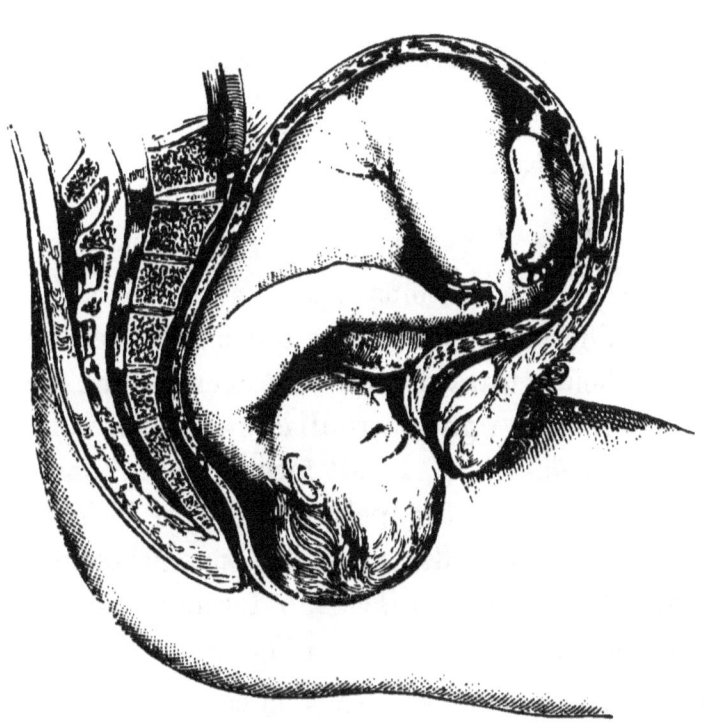

by the overlapping of the frontal bones at their suture. It has been likewise stated that at the moment of expulsion the perineum is put much more on the stretch, and is in more danger of rupture, because the occipito-frontal diameter of the child's head (which, in the occipito-anterior presentation, is in relation with the antero-posterior diameter of the pelvic outlet) is much longer than the trachelo-bregmatic, which is in apposition with it in ordinary cases. Here, again, no account is taken of the great capability which the occipito-frontal diameter has of being lessened by the overlapping of the parietal and frontal bones at the coronal suture. In fact, in most instances of occipito-posterior presentation, this shortening actually takes place to a great extent, so that the head is at first so much altered in shape as to be nearly round; whereas, in the occipito-anterior presentations, the head becomes materially lengthened, especially when the labour is at all protracted.

Should the head be arrested in the cavity of the pelvis for some hours, or should there be unusual difficulty in any of these cases, the student ought to send for assistance, as the forceps will probably be required.

Face Presentations—Mechanism.

22. Face presentations occur about once in 231 cases.* The right cheek-bone ordinarily presents; the forehead being towards the left acetabulum, and the chin towards the right sacro-iliac synchondrosis. (See Part III., *Fig.* 16.) In all face presentations, as the head passes out of the pelvis, the chin makes a turn from behind forwards, so as to emerge beneath the arch of the pubes, whilst the forehead and vertex sweep over the perineum. (*Fig.* 9.)

The ordinary face presentation is, in fact, nothing more than the ordinary presentation of the vertex, with the head extended instead of flexed upon the body.

Diagnosis of Face Presentations.

23. The face can scarcely be confounded with any other presentation except the breech, and that only

---

* Fo these statistics see Dr. Churchill's "Midwifery."

when the parts are swollen from protracted labour. You may recognize the face, before the membranes are

FIG. 9.

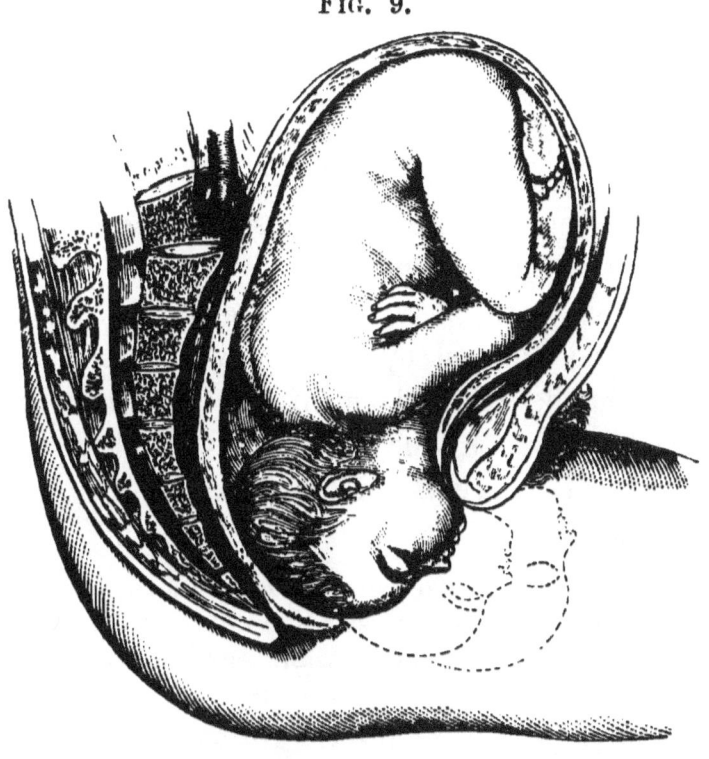

ruptured, by the hard prominences of the malar bone, forehead, bridge of the nose, and rim of the orbit. After the membranes are ruptured, you can feel the openings of the nostrils and mouth, and you can also feel within the mouth the tongue and gums. By the presence of these organs, you at once distinguish the mouth from the anus; as well as by the absence of meconial discharge, &c. (See 26, Part II.)

If a face presentation be suspected, the part should be examined with gentleness and care. Instances are related in which cheeks have been flayed, and even eyes "gouged out," by the finger-nails of rough, awkward examiners.

When the child is born, the face is generally much disfigured; for if the second stage be at all protracted, the presenting cheek and eyelids become greatly swollen and discoloured from ecchymosis.

Management of Face Presentations.

24. As a general rule, face presentations require no interference. The labour may be longer and more difficult than with a vertex presentation, but will ultimately be finished by the natural efforts. If the head should be arrested, or if the chin should not come round beneath the pubic arch, the forceps or vectis may be required. In such a case you should send for assistance.

The diameters of the face are not longer than those of the vertex; but the axes are not so well adapted to those of the pelvis, nor is the face so compressible as the vertex.

Breech Presentations—Mechanism.

25. The breech presents about once in 59 cases. The body of the child is placed obliquely in the pelvis, with the back either in front, towards the right or left acetabulum, or behind, towards the right or left sacro-iliac synchondrosis. The child is expelled with one side behind the pubic arch, and the other in front of the perineum; and, in favourable cases, the head turns so as to bring the face into the hollow of the sacrum.

In its natural position, the fœtus *in utero* bears some resemblance in shape to an egg, the head forming the large and the nates the small end. On this account a presentation of the latter at first meets with less resistance than one of the former. In such a case, therefore, the first part of the labour should on no account be hastened, but should rather be retarded, so as to give the soft parts ample time to dilate.

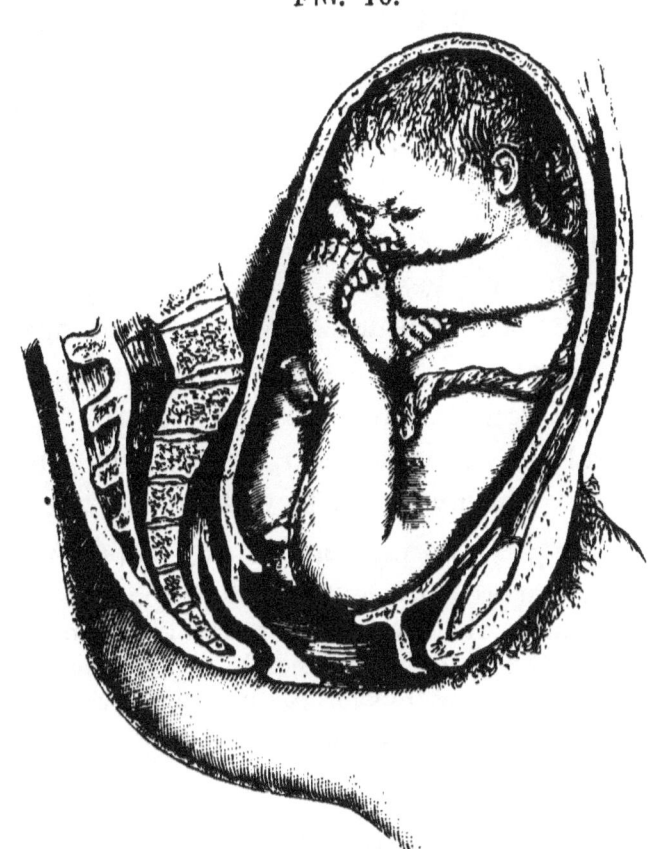

In a proper breech presentation, the legs are so flexed upon the abdomen that the feet are at first out of reach.

In the most frequent position of the breech, the left ischium of the child presents, and corresponds to the right acetabulum of the mother; the back of the child being directed forwards and to the left. (*Fig.* 10.) In fact it is merely an inversion of the ordinary position.

Diagnosis of Breech Presentations.

26. You may recognize a breech presentation before the membranes are ruptured, if you can distinguish the cleft between the buttocks and one or both tubera ischii, and especially if you can make out the pointed prominence of the coccyx in the centre. If you can reach high enough, you may feel the femur and recognize it by its great length. You may also be able to feel the very characteristic prominence of the anterior superior spinous process of the ilium, and to pass your finger into the angle between it and the femur. After the membranes are ruptured, you can distinguish the parts of generation, and meconium will escape from the anus. If you introduce your finger into the anus, you can feel the sphincter ani contracting, and the finger, when withdrawn, will be soiled with meconium.

The tuber ischii forms a hard, blunt projection in the centre of the soft cushion presented by the buttock.

In male children the scrotum occasionally becomes enormously swollen from œdema, produced by compression between the thighs. The tumour thus formed may prove very puzzling to the young accoucheur, if not previously aware of the circumstance.

Cases in which no Interference is necessary.

27. Breech cases, although more tedious than those where the vertex presents, are not usually dangerous to the mother. But there is much danger to the child from compression of the cord by the head whilst passing through the pelvis. Still, if the patient be

not a primipara, if the labour be rapid, and the child favourably situated (that is, with its back in front, and its head and arms flexed upon its body), such cases may terminate well, without any kind of manual interference.

In no instance, perhaps, is so much mischief produced by meddlesome midwifery, as in breech presentations; and yet these are the very cases in which an ignorant midwife, rejoiced at having something to pull at, would drag down the lower extremities under the idea of forwarding the labour. The result is, that time is not allowed for the soft parts to dilate. If traction be made between the pains, the child's arms, previously flexed across the chest, are carried above the head; the chin hitches upon the brim of the pelvis, and a favourable position of the head is thus changed into an extremely unfavourable one: great delay is thereby produced, and the child's life in all probability is sacrificed.

Cases for Interference.

28. In most breech presentations, some interference is necessary, but not until the lower half of the body is expelled. The danger to the child then commences. If, therefore, the upper half do not speedily follow, the labour must be hastened. As soon as you can reach the umbilicus, you may pull down some of the cord, in order to relax it, and then place the rest in the hollow of the sacrum, where it will be more out of the way of pressure. Then wrap the child's body in flannel, grasp its hips firmly, and hasten its expulsion by steady traction *during* the pains. If the child's back be situated posteriorly, you must rotate the trunk,

between the pains, so as to bring that part round to the front.

A convulsive starting of the child's limbs will sometimes indicate the approach of asphyxia from pressure on the cord. When such a symptom is noticed, there is an urgent necessity

Fig. 11.

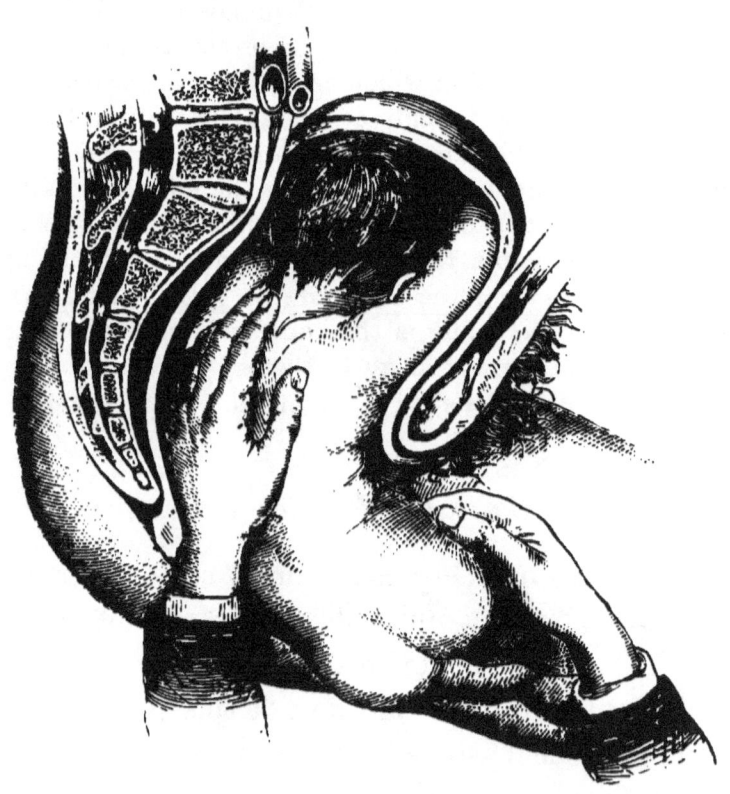

for immediate delivery. In breech presentations, the patient's friends* should be informed that the child is not presenting rightly, and that in consequence its life will be in danger, but that she herself will not incur any additional risk, nor will there be any necessity for turning the child.

---

* It is perhaps better not to inform the patient herself.

How to bring down Arms.

29. If the arms are above the head, they must be brought down; and it is generally easier to bring down the posterior arm first. For this purpose, pass two fingers over the shoulder from the back, and depress the arm obliquely downwards and forwards across the chest. Then bring down the anterior arm in a similar manner. (*Fig.* 11.)

If attempts are made to bring down the arm in an opposite direction to that indicated, the elbow will in all probability hitch upon the brim of the pelvis, and the force being exerted at right angles with the humerus, that bone will almost inevitably be fractured.

How to bring down Head.

30. If the face be in front, and the chin much raised from the chest, the position of the head must be changed. Pass the first two fingers of the left hand into the mouth, and press the chin backwards towards the sacrum, and downwards towards the chest of the child. (*Fig.* 12.) Then pass two fingers of the other hand behind the occiput, grasp the head between both hands, and extract it first downwards and backwards in the axis of the brim, and then downwards and forwards in the axis of the outlet of the pelvis. If the child be in a state of suspended animation after birth, the proper means for restoring it should be had recourse to. (See 53 and 54, Part II.)

When the chin is much raised, the longest diameter of the head, viz., the occipito-mental, corresponds to one of the diameters of the pelvis. By depressing the chin we substitute a shorter diameter, such as the trachelo-bregmatic, or at all events the occipital-frontal.

When the chin is towards the front of the pelvis, it is very likely to hitch over the pubis, and thus prevent the expulsion of the head.

Should there be unusual difficulty in extracting the head, that object may sometimes be attained by moving both arms simultaneously in the direction of the dotted line in Figure 12, whilst an assistant makes pressure on the abdomen just above the pubis.

If the nose can be reached, it will be found that by placing the two fingers, one on each side of it, and depressing the upper maxilla, the head can be acted upon more powerfully than by passing them into the mouth.

Presentation of Feet or Knees.

31. The inferior extremities, that is, the feet or knees, present about once in 105 cases. The feet may present in two ways, either with the toes turned backwards or forwards, the former being the most common. When the feet or knees present, they do not dilate the soft parts so well as the breech. The first part of the labour is consequently likely to be quicker than in a breech presentation, but the last part more lingering. Hence there is a greater danger to the child; but, in other respects, the mechanism of the labour is similar.

Foot Presentations—Diagnosis.

32. The foot can scarcely be mistaken for any other part except the hand. If you can only reach the toes, you may distinguish them from the fingers by the following peculiarities:—The toes are much shorter, and consequently cannot be doubled up like the fingers. The great toe is close to the others, and of the same length, whereas the thumb is shorter than the fingers, and widely separated from them. If you can reach the ankle, you feel the heel and malleoli; you also find that the foot is thicker than the hand, and is articulated at right angles with the leg, whereas the hand is

in a direct line with the forearm. If the membranes be ruptured, and especially if both feet can be felt, a mistake is scarcely possible.

It is of the greatest consequence in these cases that a correct diagnosis should be formed before the water escape. At the same time, too much care cannot be taken lest the membranes be ruptured in making the necessary examination.

Knee Presentations—Diagnosis.

33. The knee bears more resemblance to the elbow than to any other part; but it is larger and rounder than the elbow, and you can feel a depression between the two elevations formed by the condyles of the femur. On the contrary, you recognize the elbow by the pointed projection of olecranon between the condyles of the humerus. But all doubt is removed if you can reach the foot or the breech, and especially if both knees present.

It is scarcely possible that both elbows should present at once, but very likely that both knees should do so.

Management of Knee or Footling Cases.

34. Knee or footling cases must be managed in the same way as breech presentations, except that there is still more reason for delaying the first part of the labour. If one foot or one knee present, you should not attempt to bring down the other, because a larger dilating body is presented if you allow the limb to remain flexed upon the trunk.

Compound Presentations.

35. It sometimes happens that two different parts of the body present, forming what is called a compound presentation : thus the hand may present with the head, the breech, or the foot. The hand is known by the signs enumerated above. (See 32, Part II.) Great care is necessary in examining ; for the head or breech may be pushed up, or the arm pulled down, through ignorance or inadvertence.

Should the arm become completely engaged in the pelvis, and should the other presenting part recede, the presentation becomes one of the most unfavourable with which the accoucheur has to deal.

Management of Presentations of Hand with Head.

36. When the hand comes down before the head, there is generally more room in the pelvis than usual, and therefore you need be in no hurry to interfere. When the head is fully engaged in the cavity of the pelvis, you may make a cautious attempt to push the hand above it. If there be any difficulty in doing this, you may let it remain ; for, in all probability, it will merely have the effect of somewhat retarding the labour. Should, however, the head become arrested, you had better send for assistance, as the forceps may be required.

Presentations of the hand with the head are more frequent in premature deliveries than in labours at full term.

Treatment of Presentations of Hand with Breech or Foot.

37. When the hand presents with the breech, the case should be treated as an ordinary breech presentation. If it present with the foot, the foot should be drawn down, so as to convert the case into a presentation of the inferior extremities.

In presentations of the hand and foot the cord frequently prolapses. The safety of the child then requires that the labour should be terminated without delay.

Plural Births.

38. "Plural Births" are those in which more than one fœtus is expelled. Twins occur about once in 81 cases. Cases of three or more at a birth are exceedingly rare. Twin children are nearly always below the average size; they are generally enclosed in separate membranous bags; the placentæ also are distinct, although usually united by their edges. In the majority of cases the heads of both children present, but it is almost as common to find the head of one and the breech or feet of the other presenting. In some rare cases there is only one common placenta.

The mortality amongst twins, and especially triplets or quadruplets, is greater than amongst other children, from the circumstance that these labours are more often premature than others, and also that the children are smaller and less vigorous.

Mechanism of Twin Labours.

39. The delivery of the first child is usually more tedious than an ordinary labour, but the delivery of the second is much more speedy. In most cases there is an interval of rest between the birth of the first and second child, which may vary from five minutes to half an hour or more. The membranes of the second child do not give way until after the birth of the first; the two placentæ are expelled after the birth of the second child.

The delivery of the first child is slow, from the circumstance that much power is lost, because a considerable portion of the uterine pressure is transmitted indirectly, through the medium of the bag of the waters enclosing the second child. The delivery of the second child is speedy, because the soft parts are well dilated by the passage of the first.

The period of repose between the birth of the first and second child has been known to last for several hours, and even days. Dr. Merriman relates a case in which the second child was retained for six weeks.

Diagnosis of Twins.

40. Before labour commences there is no certain sign by which you can ascertain the presence of twins, with the exception, perhaps, of that which is derived from the auscultation of two distinct fœtal hearts. After the first child is born the nature of the case is obvious: if you place your hand on the abdomen, the uterus feels tense, hard, and but a little diminished in size; if you examine *per vaginam*, you at once distin-

guish the bag containing the presenting part of the second child.

Before labour, the size of the abdomen is a very fallacious sign of the presence of twins, for it may depend on other causes, such as excess of liquor amnii, &c. But if two distinct bodies can be felt through the parietes, with a sulcus between them, it is very probable that the uterus contains twins. The evidence amounts almost to certainty if, on applying the stethoscope to two parts of the abdomen remote from one another, the sound of the fœtal heart is heard distinctly in each situation. The fœtal heart gives a double sound, which very much resembles a muffled ticking, such as is heard when a watch is placed beneath a pillow. The beats of the fœtal heart bear no fixed relation in frequency to those of the mother's, but in general there are at least twice as many in a given time. The discrimination of these sounds requires a quiet room and a practised ear; the student should therefore take every opportunity of making himself familiar with them.

Management of Twin Cases.

41. The delivery of the first child is to be managed in the same way as an ordinary labour. As soon as it is born and separated from the mother, apply a binder round the abdomen, and wait for the expulsion of the second child. Do not attempt to remove the placenta of the first child until after the birth of the second. When this has taken place, the two placentæ will be expelled together. If they remain in the vagina, twist the cords together and remove them in the manner directed in 39, Part I.

An alarming hæmorrhage might ensue if the first placenta were forcibly separated before the birth of the second child, as a large bleeding surface would be thereby exposed, at a time when the uterus would be incapable of close contraction.

The binder is especially necessary in twin cases, because the bleeding surface, which is exposed by the separation of the placentæ, is twice as large as in an ordinary case. Moreover, the uterus, in consequence of previous over-distension, is more likely to fall into a state of inertia when the labour is over.

Inaction of Uterus after Birth of First Child.

42. Sometimes the uterus remains in a state of inaction for a considerable period after the birth of the first child. Should there be no pains within half an hour, you may tighten the bandage, and rupture the membranes. Should there be none within an hour, you may give ergot, as directed in 10, Part II., provided the presentation is natural. If the second child be not born within an hour and a half, you had better send for assistance.

Authors are somewhat divided in opinion as to the treatment of these cases: some recommend immediate interference, whilst others advise that they should be left entirely to nature; the majority, however, are in favour of a middle course. It is not well to interfere too soon after the birth of the first child, because the woman may be somewhat exhausted, and may need a little repose. At the same time, it is not advisable to delay interference too long, *e.g.*, for several hours, because the soft parts, which have been well dilated by the first child, will have time to contract, and thus any operation (such as turning or the application of the forceps) which may be required will be rendered much more difficult. If there are symptoms of exhaustion after the birth of the second child, a table-spoonful of brandy may be given, together with ℔xxx. of tinct. opii.

In all twin cases, when the first child is born, the patient should be informed that she is likely to give birth to a second.

This should not be told to her abruptly, and at the same time she should be cheered by the assurance that in all probability she will not have to go through one-tenth part of the suffering which she has already endured.

Tedious Labour from Disproportion between Head and Pelvis.

43. The second stage of labour may be retarded by a slight disproportion between the size of the head and pelvis: thus the former may be larger than usual, and the latter somewhat contracted, either at its brim, cavity, or outlet. If the disproportion be not great, the uterine efforts will probably overcome the resistance, after some hours of additional suffering, without any bad result to either mother or child.

The pelvis may be too small in all its proportions, or it may be irregular in consequence of disease. (See 13, Part III.)

A very large and firmly ossified fœtal head may be a cause of difficult labour, especially when the pelvis is not roomy: this cause is more often met with in male than female children.

When such Cases may be left to Nature.

44. Cases of tedious labour from want of room in the pelvis require much time and patience, and should not be hastily interfered with. You may safely leave them to nature, so long as the general condition of the woman is good, the pains being regular and powerful, and the head advancing ever so little in a given time;

the passages being neither hot nor tender, and the pulse not rising above 100 between the pains.

One of the first lessons which the young accoucheur has to learn is patience. Patience enables the adept, who knows by experience what pangs nature will endure at such times, and yet in the end accomplish her work safely, to quietly await the result, when the tyro, listening to the suggestions of his own timorous imagination, and to the entreaties of the woman and her friends, would rashly resort to instruments, and perhaps sacrifice the lives of the mother and her helpless offspring.

The student should take care not to mistake the elongation of the cranium and swelling of the scalp, which are so marked in difficult labours, for an advance of the head.

Retention of Urine during Labour.

45. In tedious labours, the pressure of the head upon the bladder may cause retention of urine. If there be any doubt as to the woman's ability to pass water, you should draw it off. For this purpose, an elastic male catheter is preferable to the ordinary instrument. The woman lying on her left side, feel for the meatus urinarius with the tip of the left forefinger. You will find it beneath the pubic arch, and just above the vaginal orifice, from which it is separated by a slight projection. Then introduce the catheter (previously oiled), push it on into the bladder, and receive the urine in a small basin. If the child's head resist the catheter, you must repress it a little with your fingers.

Nurses are very apt to confound the dribbling away of liquor amnii with passing water, and *vice versâ*. Their statements, therefore, must be received with much caution.

During labour, the urethra becomes elongated, and passes almost straight up behind the symphysis pubis. It is on this account that a long flexible catheter is preferable.

When the labour is lingering, the parts of generation may become so swollen, that it is difficult to detect the meatus urinarius. When such is the case, the parts must be exposed to view: it is better to do this than to run any risk from long-continued retention of urine.

The catheter should always be used before turning or employing instruments.

Cramps during Labour.

46. During the second stage of labour, the pressure of the head upon the sacral nerves occasionally produces very painful cramps in the thighs and legs. Delivery is the only remedy for these; but some relief may be afforded by friction of the affected limb.

Should simple friction be insufficient, the limb may be rubbed with the linimentum chloroformi.

Sometimes the pain arising from cramps is so excruciating as to render the inhalation of chloroform advisable. (See 16, Part II.)

Death of Fœtus before or during Labour.

47. The fœtus may die either before or during labour. If it die before the full term of pregnancy, it will be retained until it appears to act as a foreign body, and excites the uterus to throw it off. The time during which it thus remains may vary from a few hours to several days, or even weeks.

The death of the fœtus may be caused by intra-uterine disease, such as syphilis, &c. ; by blows, falls, or other shocks; or it may be a result of difficult labour. According to the time that the fœtus has been retained *in utero*, it may either be slightly decomposed, as shown by some discolouration and peeling of the cuticle, or it may be so putrid and rotten that it will scarcely hang together.

Signs of Death of Fœtus.

48. When the fœtus dies before labour, its movements cease to be felt, the abdomen subsides, and there is a feeling of coldness and weight in the uterine region. The breasts become flaccid, and lose the characteristic appearances of pregnancy. The woman's health suffers; her breath is offensive, and her eyes are surrounded by a dark circle. During labour, the cranial bones feel loose and movable beneath the flaccid scalp, and there is no caput succedaneum, however long the labour may have lasted. If there be much decomposition, the scalp becomes emphysematous, and crackles under the finger. The liquor amnii contains meconium; the discharges are offensive, and flatus often escapes from the uterus. But auscultation affords the surest sign, both before and during labour. If the fœtal heart has been heard distinctly, and if its pulsations, after a time, become quicker and fainter, and cease altogether, you have tolerably certain proof of the death of the fœtus.

Many of the signs first enumerated are, when taken by themselves, extremely equivocal, because they depend very much upon sensations which are apt to be fallacious. The diagnosis of the death of the fœtus may be a matter of much importance in difficult labour; for it may determine the kind of instrumental interference which is to be employed. The looseness of the cranial bones arises from the pulpy condition of the brain produced by decomposition. The emphysema of the scalp is caused by gas generated during putrefaction. When meconium escapes with the liquor amnii in a *head* presentation, it is a suspicious circumstance, as it indicates a relaxation of the sphincter ani.

Management of Delivery with Stillborn Children.

49. When the child is dead, the progress of the labour is not materially affected. The uterine action may, perhaps, be somewhat torpid, and a dose of ergot may be necessary. For some days after the labour the vagina should be well syringed with warm water, rendered disinfectant (see Note 69, Part II.), in order to wash away any putrid matters which may remain behind. This should be done once every day at least.

The absorption of any kind of putrid matter should be carefully guarded against, as it is a fertile source of puerperal fever.

For the purpose of syringing out the vagina, an india-rubber bottle, or an ordinary Higginson's enema syringe, will answer very well.

Coiling of Cord round Neck—Treatment.

50. When the child's head is born, it often happens that the cord is twisted once or twice round the neck. This is seldom a matter of much consequence, because, in these cases, the cord is generally longer than usual. You may draw down a loop of the cord, so as to relieve

its tension, and, if you can, slip it over the head. If it be too tight for this, you may slip it over the shoulders. When the cord is so unusually tight as to threaten strangulation of the infant, you may divide it, taking care immediately afterwards to secure the cut vessels by ligatures. Such a proceeding, however, is scarcely ever necessary.

The coiling of the cord around the neck or limbs appears to be a provision of nature for disposing of its superfluous length, and obviating the danger of prolapse.

If, as very seldom happens, a short cord be tightly twisted around the neck, the child is in danger of both strangulation and compression of the cord. There is also some risk of forcible detachment of the placenta, or even an inversion of the uterus.

Delay in Expulsion of Body—Treatment.

51. Sometimes there is a considerable delay after the birth of the child's head. The face becomes livid and much swollen, and the child appears in imminent danger of strangulation or apoplexy. If after ten minutes the body should not be expelled, the delivery may be assisted by making firm pressure on the fundus uteri, and using gentle traction upon the neck, or, still better, upon the trunk, by passing up the forefinger along the neck, and hooking it round the axilla.

The pressure upon the fundus uteri is made for the purpose of inducing uterine contraction, and thus obviating the danger of post-partum hæmorrhage.

Asphyxia of Infant—Causes.

52. When the child is born, it may be in a state of suspended animation from asphyxia; the heart beats, but there are no respiratory efforts. This condition may arise from various causes, such as pressure on the head during a long labour, flooding from premature detachment of the placenta, compression of the cord or neck during birth, &c.

In some instances, the condition of the child borders closely upon syncope from anæmia; such would be the result of flooding from premature detachment of the placenta. In others, there is a state of cerebral congestion approaching apoplexy, and this we should expect to find where there has been a long interval between the birth of the head and of the body, and, consequently, much pressure on the neck.

Treatment of Asphyxia.

53. If the cord pulsates, you should not, as a general rule, tie it for at least a quarter of an hour; but if the child appears to be in an apoplectic condition, as shown by great swelling and lividity of the countenance, you may at once divide the cord, and allow two or three teaspoonfuls of blood to escape from it. In all cases you may first attempt to produce respiration by exposing the face freely to the air, and sprinkling it with cold water; by wetting the trunk and limbs with brandy, and rubbing them briskly with warm flannels. You may try these means for a minute or two; but if they fail, you must have recourse to artificial respiration without delay.

The popular remedy, amongst nurses, of slapping the child's buttocks will sometimes succeed in producing respiratory effort. Galvanism is a powerful means of resuscitation, when a proper apparatus is at hand.

Other means of exciting respiration have been recommended, such as holding ammonia or burnt feathers to the nostrils, tickling the fauces with a feather, &c.

Care should always be taken, in these cases, to free the mouth or fauces from any mucus which may clog them.

The contact of cold air with the skin is a powerful stimulus to the respiratory act, and therefore the child's face should always be freely uncovered.

The limbs should be rubbed with gentle pressure upwards, in order to promote the circulation by propelling the venous blood towards the heart.

Mode of performing Artificial Respiration.

54. The most efficient means of resuscitation is undoubtedly artificial respiration. To perform this, first place the infant briskly in the prone position, so as to clear the fauces of mucus or other fluids. Then place it in a sitting posture, and alternately raise it up by the arms and set it down again, about twenty times in a minute. Each time that the child is set down the arms should be pressed gently against the sides, and the head inclined forwards. These movements should be continued until the child breathes with regularity; and they should not be abandoned as hopeless, whilst the least pulsation of the heart is perceptible.

The mode of performing artificial respiration which has been just mentioned is, with some slight modifications, the same as Dr. Silvester's, whose plan received the approval of the Medico-Chirurgical Society. It has been found to be a more effectual method of inflating the chest than that recommended by the late Dr. Marshall Hall. The latter, however, will, in many cases, answer very well, and is thus performed :—Place the infant in the prone position, make gentle pressure on the back of the thorax, and then remove that pressure, turn the child on the side and a little beyond. This should be repeated about twenty times in a minute. The child is then to be placed with the face prone, and douched rapidly with hot and cold water alternately.

The hot and cold water used for sprinkling the child should be respectively of the temperature of about 60° and 100° Fahr.

If the infant continue very feeble after resuscitation, it is a good plan to give it about five drops of brandy in half a teaspoonful of milk and water.

If, however, it should not revive, but appear likely to die, it is right, before leaving, to tell the parents of this, in order that they may not lose the opportunity of having it baptized.

The old-fashioned mode of performing artificial respiration is still preferred by some, and consists in inflation of the lungs by means of a proper tube, or, in default of it, a quill or piece of tobacco-pipe. If the tube is used, it should be inserted into the larynx. To do this, the forefinger of the left hand should be passed over the root of the tongue until it reaches the epiglottis. The end of the tube is then to be passed between the tip of the finger and the posterior surface of the epiglottis, and introduced into the rima glottidis. If a quill or tobacco-pipe is used, the child's lips are pressed around the tube and its nostrils closed ; at the same time, the larynx is pressed backwards so as to shut the œsophagus. The lungs are then inflated by alternately blowing into the mouth and depressing the ribs with the hand. Care should be taken not to inflate too forcibly, for fear of rupturing some of the pulmonary air-cells. This method, however, is inferior in efficacy to the two others, and especially to the first. It does not imitate the natural respiratory movements so closely, and it may injure the delicate tissue of an infant's lung. But yet, in any case, whenever one plan appears to fail, another may be tried.

It is sometimes necessary to continue artificial respiration for at least an hour and a half.

Post-partum Hæmorrhage, or "Flooding."

55. The flow of blood which usually accompanies the separation of the placenta may be so excessive as to produce marked constitutional symptoms. It is then called post-partum hæmorrhage, because it follows the birth of the child. The hæmorrhage is always occasioned by uterine inertia, and, if profuse, may cause pallor of the lips and face, weak, fluttering pulse, faintness, sighing respiration, dimness of sight, dysphagia, jactitation, convulsions, and death.

Post-partum hæmorrhage is always a dangerous and alarming accident, requiring prompt and vigorous treatment.

Every student who attends midwifery should know how to meet such cases when they occur. Dr. Gooch has well remarked, "In these cases, you would give anything for a consultation, but there is no time for it: the life of the patient depends on the man who is upon the spot; he must stand to his gun, and trust to his own resources. A practitioner who is not fully competent to undertake these cases of hæmorrhage can never conscientiously cross the threshold of a lying-in chamber."

In most cases of post-partum hæmorrhage, an unnatural rapidity and jerking of the pulse may be noticed, before the actual occurrence of flooding. Dr. Churchill, in his "Theory and Practice of Midwifery," has made some valuable remarks on this point. He says: "In almost all the cases of flooding after labour, when I have had an opportunity of examining the pulse up to the time of the occurrence, I have found it remain quick, and perhaps full, instead of sinking after delivery. This has been so marked in several cases, that I now never leave a patient so long as this peculiarity remains; and, in more than one instance, I believe the patient has owed her safety to this precaution. Three cases occurred within a very short time of each other, in which I noticed this undue quickness of the pulse, without any other untoward symptom; at that time there was no excessive discharge, and the uterus was well contracted. In all these, alarming hæmorrhage occurred within an hour, and was with difficulty arrested."

Symptoms of Post-partum Hæmorrhage.

56. In most cases of post-partum hæmorrhage the flooding is sufficiently obvious, both to the woman and her attendants, for the blood will gush forth upon the bed-clothes and mattress until they are saturated, and then run in a full stream on the floor. The uterus will be felt to be in a relaxed and flabby condition, so that you can scarcely define its limits; or, if it contract and harden for a few seconds, it will speedily return to its former state.

In all cases where there is any reason to apprehend hæmorrhage, the pulse should be frequently felt, and the uterus examined. The patient should be asked whether she feels any discharge running from her; and the napkin should be frequently removed and inspected.

Treatment of Post-partum Hæmorrhage.

57. In treating post-partum hæmorrhage, the chief indication is to produce uterine contraction. For this purpose, grasp the uterus firmly with one or both

hands, and keep up the pressure for a considerable period. Apply frequently cold wet cloths, or a bladder containing ice, to the vulva, hypogastrium, and thighs, or introduce a lump of ice into the upper part of the vagina. Keep the woman's head low by taking away the pillows, and remove all the clothes, except a sheet, from the lower part of her body. Give a full dose of ergot immediately. This may be followed in a quarter of an hour by a table-spoonful of oil of turpentine. If there be much tendency to syncope, open the windows, and give stimulants, such as brandy, ether, or sal-volatile. Do not leave the woman for at least three hours after the birth of the child, or until the uterus *remains* well contracted. Before leaving, give an opiate to tranquillize the nervous system. Also place a good-sized compress upon the uterus, and apply a binder firmly round the abdomen.

Before adopting the treatment above described, it may be better to place the patient on her back; because in that position the uterus can be more fully commanded, and pressure more effectually applied than when she is lying on her side.

If the uterus do not contract when grasped, it may be pressed and kneaded by the hands, in various ways, or friction may be made on its surface, through the loose abdominal parietes.

The cloths may be wetted with vinegar and water. The more suddenly they are applied the better. When, however, ice can be procured, there is no mode of applying cold so effectual as that of passing up a lump of ice, the size of a small hen's egg, as far as, or even within, the os uteri.

℥j. of the extractum ergotæ liquid. may be given at once in these cases. If the woman be a multipara, who has previously suffered from post-partum hæmorrhage, it is an excellent plan to give the ergot shortly before the birth of the child. Hæmorrhage may be thus entirely prevented.

It is a good plan to inject ergotin subcutaneously, when we wish to obtain the effect of ergot very speedily, or when, as often happens, the ergot is rejected by vomiting. The needle of the hypodermic syringe should be inserted deeply into the integument covering the glutæus muscle.

The oil of turpentine may be given with an equal proportion of milk.

A table-spoonful of brandy, or a teaspoonful of sal-volatile, may be given at a time. The sal-volatile may be given either in milk or water.

The dose of opium should be about ♏xxx. of the tincture.

One of the best compresses which can be used in these cases is a large old-fashioned pin-cushion, such as is often seen in lying-in rooms garnished with "Welcome, little stranger," or some other appropriate device, in pins. After carefully ridding it of all pins and needles, the cushion may be turned to good account in the way mentioned. In default of it, two or three folded napkins, or a small thick book, may be used.

Should the means above recommended be not successful in speedily checking the hæmorrhage, the student should send for assistance without delay.

There are several other methods of inducing uterine contraction, in case the above expedients do not answer. Some of them require, however, much skill, and would be attended with considerable risk in the hands of an inexperienced student. Amongst the safe and simple ones may be mentioned the application of the child to the breast, an expedient which was strongly recommended by Dr. Rigby. A contraction of the uterus is produced from the sympathy between that organ and the mamma.

Another safe and simple remedy, is the cold douche. As Dr. Marshall Hall has shown it is a very powerful means of exciting reflex uterine contraction. The abdomen being uncovered, a stream of cold water is to be poured on the hypogastrium from a considerable height, by means of a jug.

Injections of cold water into the rectum will frequently succeed in arresting uterine hæmorrhage.

Compression of the abdominal aorta has been resorted to with success.

The next class of remedies to be mentioned act directly upon the inner surface of the uterus, but their employment is somewhat risky in inexperienced hands.

The first of these, the introduction of the hand into the uterus, will sometimes excite that organ to contract when other means fail. When the hand is in the uterus, it may be moved about, so as to increase the stimulus occasioned by its presence. The bleeding vessels may also be compressed between the knuckles of that hand and the palm of the other, placed on the outside of the abdomen.

This proceeding may be adopted when others fail, but it is attended with some risk of inflammation.

Injections into the uterine cavity are powerful remedies, but require considerable care to insure safety.

Injections of cold or hot water will excite the uterus to strong reflex action.

When the patient is flushed, and the pulse bounding, an injection of iced water, as recommended by Dr. Tyler Smith, is a powerful hæmostatic.

When, however, the patient is already cold, collapsed, and exhausted, the injection of hot water into the uterus (which was first introduced into this country by Dr. Attlhill, of Dublin) is far preferable. The water should be about 110° Fahr. in temperature.

But the most powerful remedy of all, because it both excites uterine contraction and causes thrombosis, or coagulation of blood in the uterine sinuses, we owe to Dr. Robert Barnes. This is the injection of perchloride of iron into the uterus. He uses a solution consisting of four ounces of the liquor ferri perchloridi of the British Pharmacopœia, with twelve ounces of water. This should be thrown up by means of a Higginson's syringe and long elastic tube.

When a battery is at hand, galvanism may be tried. It will sometimes overcome uterine inertia, when all other means have failed.

Lastly, women have been saved, when in imminent danger of death from hæmorrhage, by the operation of transfusion, which consists in abstracting blood from the vein of a healthy person, and injecting it into the vein of the patient. But this is a delicate operation, and attended with some danger, and therefore, like some of those just mentioned, ought not to be attempted without a consultation.

Internal Hæmorrhage—Diagnosis.

58. In some instances, which are not very common, there is no external hæmorrhage, but the bleeding takes place internally, into the cavity of the uterus. The usual symptoms of hæmorrhage appear, but without discharge of blood. The uterus swells, and becomes almost as large as if it contained a second child; but, at the same time, feels soft and doughy, and not firm and hard like a uterus containing a child. On examining, you find its cavity filled with fluid blood and coagula.

In internal hæmorrhage, the os uteri is closed by the detached placenta, by a coagulum, or by a circular constriction of its fibres, &c.

Treatment of Internal Hæmorrhage.

59. In internal hæmorrhage, the first indication is to facilitate the flow of blood through the os uteri, and the next to insure uterine contraction. To accomplish the first, introduce your hand into the uterus, and remove the detached placenta, or any large coagula

which may obstruct the opening of the os. Then use the means for producing uterine contraction, which have been before described.

In all cases of post-partum hæmorrhage, the placenta should be removed when detached, whether it be in the uterus or vagina.

When the woman is in the ordinary position, the left hand will be found the most convenient for introduction into the uterus, because it is better adapted to the curve of the sacrum.

Those clots only ought to be removed which are detached, and in the lower part of the uterus. The removal of clots which are adherent to the uterine parietes would be very likely to cause a great increase of flooding.

After-Pains.

60. Women, after delivery, are liable to painful contractions of the uterus, which are called "after-pains." These are very common in multiparæ, but comparatively rare in primiparæ. They come on immediately after the expulsion of the placenta, and may continue for many hours, or even for one or two days. They recur at intervals, like labour pains, and often serve to expel coagula and other matters from the uterus.

Although after-pains occasion much suffering, they seldom give rise to any fever, or abdominal tenderness. The woman feels quite easy between each pain. The suffering produced by them is borne with much impatience, from a belief that they do no good. This idea is not strictly correct, as they are frequently caused by efforts which the uterus makes to get rid of clots, or portions of membrane remaining in its cavity. Nevertheless, it is certain that in some of the worst cases of after-pains no such cause can be detected.

Treatment of After-Pains.

61. As a general rule, after-pains should not be checked in any way for at least six hours after delivery; if by that time they continue with unabated severity, and seem likely to prevent sleep, you should give an opiate, and this may be repeated every six hours if necessary. Warm fomentations to the abdomen are also of service.

Should the uterus feel larger and harder than usual, there is in all probability something within its cavity which it is endeavouring to throw off. An examination may therefore be made, and if any clot or portion of membrane be detected by the finger, it should be removed. Purgative enemata are of much service in promoting the expulsion of clots.

In order to check after-pains, ♏xv. of tinct. opii may be given at a time, in ʒj. of mist. camph.

The most convenient kind of warm fomentation is the application of large flannels wrung out of hot water. These should be covered over with dry flannels, or, what is better, a piece of oiled silk or sheet gutta-percha. A large piece of spongio-piline will answer the same purpose very well.

Nervous Shock after Delivery.

62. Some women, especially those of hysterical temperament, show symptoms of a severe nervous shock after delivery. They appear much exhausted, and are liable to attacks of syncope. There is often severe headache, and much intolerance of light and sound.

The pulse is soft and compressible; sometimes slower, but much more frequently faster than usual. The countenance is pale and anxious, the tongue moist and tolerably clean, the skin soft and perspirable.

When the headache depends upon constipation or disordered bowels, the tongue will be coated with fur, and very probably red at its tips and edges.

Should it depend upon any inflammatory affection of the abdominal organs, the secretions of milk and lochia will be checked.

Should there be much tendency to syncope, a stethoscopic examination of the heart should be made, to ascertain whether there is any organic disease of that organ.

Treatment of Nervous Shock.

63. When there is a severe nervous shock after delivery, the best remedy is an opiate combined with a diffusible stimulant; and this may be repeated, if necessary, in smaller doses every four hours. The most perfect repose should be enjoined. The head should be placed rather lower than usual, and the horizontal posture strictly maintained.

The following draught will answer the purpose very well:—

℞ Liq. Morphiæ Hydrochlor., ♏xxx.
 Spt. Ammon. Arom., ʒss.
 Aq. Camph. ad ℥iss.
 M. ft. Haustus statim sumend.

Or this:—

℞ Liq. Morphiæ Acetat., ♏xxx.
 Træ. Sumbul., ♏xx.
 Spt. Chloroform., ♏x.
 Aq. Camph. ad ℥iss.
 M. ft. Haustus statim sumend.

Sleeplessness after Delivery.

64. Women of a nervous, excitable temperament are sometimes troubled with insomnia or sleeplessness after delivery. This requires absolute repose and quiet; tea and coffee should be forbidden, and an opiate or a dose of hydrate of chloral administered; or, in slight cases, bromide of potassium or ammonium.

The following will be found to be a good form of opiate:—

  ℞ Liq. Morphiæ Acet., ♏xxx.
    Spt. Chloroform., ♏x.
    Aq. Camph., ʒiss.
  M. ft. Haust. horâ somni sumend.

Hydrate of chloral is often a more effectual remedy for insomnia than opium, and does not leave, like opium, unpleasant after-affects.

It may be given as recommended in 11, Part II.

The bromides may be thus administered:—

  ℞ Potassii Bromid., gr. x.
    Ammonii, gr. v.
    Spt. Chloroform., ♏x.
    Aq. Camph., ʒiss.
  M. ft. Haust. horâ somni sumend.

Retention of Urine after Delivery—Treatment.

65. Retention of urine is sometimes a consequence of a tedious labour, and arises from swelling of the vaginal orifice and meatus urinarius, together with some loss of power in the bladder. You may first try the application of warm fomentations to the vulva; if these do not produce the desired effect, you must use the catheter. If the inability to pass water continue, tonics and diuretics should be given.

The following mixture may be administered in these cases :—

℞ Tinct. Ferri Perchlorid.,
  Spt. Æth. Nit., āā ʒj.
  Aquam ad ʒviij.
  M. Capt. sextam partem ter die.

Sometimes when the patient has been weakened by tedious labour or flooding, there will be inability to pass water so long as she remains in the supine position; but a slight change of position, such as elevating the shoulders (if not otherwise improper), or turning on the elbow and knees, will suffice to overcome the difficulty.

Incontinence of Urine after Delivery—Treatment.

66. Incontinence of urine is occasionally a result of tedious labour, and is caused by temporary paralysis of the sphincter vesicæ from long-continued pressure. If the power of retaining the urine be not recovered in a few days, preparations of iron or other tonics should be given.

The following formula is a suitable one :—

℞ Træ. Cantharidis,
  Træ. Ferri Perchlor., āā ʒj.
  Syrupi, ʒij.
  Aquæ, ʒviiss.
  M. Sumat. sextam partem ter die.

Should this fail, the following mixture may be had recourse to :—

℞ Liquor Strychniæ, ♏xxx.
  Syrupi, ʒij.
  Træ. Ferri Perchlor., ʒij.
  Aquæ, ʒviiss.
  M. Capt. sextam partem bis die.

The author has found this mixture of the greatest service

both in retention and incontinence of urine arising from loss of power in the bladder after delivery.

Incontinence of urine sometimes arises from sloughing of the base of the bladder after very severe labour. Incontinence from this cause does not come on immediately after delivery, and is generally preceded by much local pain, tenderness, and fœtid discharge, accompanied with considerable fever and constitutional irritation. When such symptoms are present, the student should request a consultation.

Deficiency of Lochial Discharge—Treatment.

67. The lochial discharge may be deficient in quantity, or may entirely disappear within two or three days after delivery. This is not unusual after the birth of stillborn children, and need occasion no alarm, provided it be unaccompanied with febrile symptoms. The treatment is to apply warm fomentations to the vulva, and syringe the vagina daily with warm water.

Suppression of the lochia is one of the symptoms of puerperal fever, and is then an effect rather than a cause of constitutional disturbance.

Excessive Lochial Discharge—Treatment.

68. In other cases the lochia may be excessive in quantity, or may last beyond the usual time, producing much debility. The proper treatment is to enjoin rest, and to give tonics, such as quinine and iron. In some cases ergot of rye is of great service; in others, astringent injections are of much use.

Sulphate of quinine may be given in two-grain doses with mx. of acid. sulph. dil. to each dose. Of the preparations of iron, the tincture of the perchloride answers the best, and may be given in ♏x. doses twice a day. Weak injections of sulphate of zinc and alum are the most suitable. Decoctions of oak-bark or tormentilla will also answer very well. Too much exercise within the first fortnight or three weeks after delivery may cause the red discharge to return, and even to put on a hæmorrhagic character (See 70, Part II.), after having lost its colour and almost disappeared. When this happens, the patient should be kept perfectly quiet in the horizontal posture, and should take five grains of powdered ergot of rye three times a day.

Offensive Lochial Discharge—Treatment.

69. In other cases the quality of the lochia is altered, the colour being dark, and the odour very offensive. This may depend upon the presence of putrid matter in the uterus, such as decomposed portions of placenta, clots, &c. The vagina should be syringed two or three times a day with warm water or with weak disinfectant lotions.

Putrid and decomposing matters within the uterus are a fertile source of phlegmasia dolens, or even puerperal fever. (See 36, 37, and 38, Part III.) They ought, therefore, to be carefully removed. The patient should be directed to pass water when resting on the elbows and knees, as clots, &c., will more readily come away in that position, because the vagina and outlet of the pelvis are then directed downwards.

But if there be the slightest apprehension of septicæmia, syringing should also be employed. Although the operation of syringing the vagina is one which every well-instructed nurse ought to be able to perform, yet it will often be found that, if this most important measure be simply ordered and left to the nurse, it will be carried out most ineffectually. If, therefore, there be any doubt on this point, the medical attendant would do well to use the syringe himself in the first instance, and thus instruct the nurse as to her future duties.

The best instrument for the purpose is an ordinary Higginson's enema-syringe with elastic vaginal tube. Having placed the patient on her back, with a bed-pan under her hips (for this purpose the slipper-shaped pans are the best), and separated the thighs, the vaginal tube is to be passed up as far as the os uteri, and the injection thrown up in a full stream. In some cases it may be advisable to wash out the cavity of the uterus; but as this is an operation requiring much tact and attended with some risk, the student had better not undertake it without assistance. For a disinfectant injection, a pint of warm water should be used, with the addition of two or three teaspoonfuls either of the liquor potassæ permanganatis or of the glycerinum acidi carbolici.

Secondary Hæmorrhage—Causes.

70. Secondary hæmorrhage is a sudden loss of blood from the uterus, occurring some hours after delivery, or even at any period within the month. It is most usually caused by the retention of a portion of adherent placenta, or of a large clot, in the uterus; but it may arise from uterine relaxation, disturbance of the circulation, laceration or disease of the uterus, &c.

In all these cases a careful investigation should be made, to ascertain, if possible, the cause of the hæmorrhage. For instance, the history of the case, and the undue size of the uterus, may lead to suspicion of retained portions of the placenta or clots; to make sure of this a careful vaginal examination should be made.

Secondary Hæmorrhage—Treatment.

71. The treatment of secondary hæmorrhage must depend very much on the cause. Portions of placenta

or clots should be removed, if possible; and the hæmorrhage should be restrained by cold applications, cold enemata, and astringents, and by giving ergot of rye, turpentine, and Indian hemp.

When the hæmorrhage is copious and severe, ergot of rye and turpentine may be thus given :—

   ℞ Ext. Ergot. Liquid., ʒj.
    Aq. Cinnam. ad ʒiij.
   M. Capt. tertiam partem omni horâ.

After this has been taken, turpentine may be administered as follows :—

   ℞ Ol. Terebinth., ʒj.
    Mucilag., q.s.
    Syrupi, ʒj.
    Aquam ad ʒvj.
   M. Sumat 6tam partem ter die.

But if the hæmorrhage be more chronic in character, the following mixtures may be given :—

   ℞ Ext. Ergot. Liquid., ʒij.
    Ol. Terebinth., ʒj.
    Mucilag., q.s.
    Aquam ad ʒviij.
   M. Capt. 8vam partem ter die.

Or the following :—

   ℞ Ext. Ergot. Liquid., ʒij.
    Træ. Cannab. Indic., ʒiss.
    Aq. Cinnam. ad ʒviij.
   M. Capt. 8vam partem ter die.

A vaginal injection of half a pint of infusion of matico may be used in bad cases, or the uterine cavity may be swabbed with liq. ferri perchlorid., by means of a sponge of the size of a walnut, which has been firmly attached to a piece of whalebone. This should be passed up through a large-sized Fergusson's speculum.

Lacerated Perineum.

72. Slight lacerations of the perineum, which merely pass through the thin anterior edge of the mucous membrane, or fourchette, are very common, especially in first labours, and give rise to little or no inconvenience. But sometimes the laceration extends further, passing through the whole substance of the perineum, even as far as the sphincter ani. In other cases, happily by no means common, the rent passes through the sphincter ani, and sometimes even the recto-vaginal septum, laying the vagina and rectum open into one passage.

The fourchette is almost always lacerated in first labours, without any subsequent inconvenience being occasioned.

A laceration of the perineum, properly so-called, seldom heals by the first intention, if unattended to, because the wound is kept open by the constant passage of the discharges over it, as well as by the action of the sphincter ani. When the laceration extends through the recto-vaginal septum, the patient loses the power of retaining her fæces, which are liable to come away, at any time, involuntarily. Her after-condition is consequently most deplorable. In such a case it would be well to send for assistance.

Lacerated Perineum—Treatment.

73. Slight lacerations of the perineum require little or no treatment. It will generally be enough to keep the parts clean, to direct the woman to lie on her side, and to tie the knees together. When more severe they should be treated at once, so as to insure, if possible, union by the first intention. The edges of

the wound should be brought together by three or four sutures of silver wire or silk.

The interrupted suture is the best for ordinary use, and silver wire is, in the opinion of the author, preferable to silk. The best form of needle is Hagedorn's modification of the old-fashioned semicircular one. (See Note 2, Part I.) The following is the most convenient mode of operating:—After the placenta has been expelled, and the uterus has become well contracted, place the patient across the bed, on her left side, with her nates close to the edge, and opposite to the light from a window or a candle placed on a chair. Let the thighs be well flexed upon the body, with the knees separated by a pillow, and let them be kept steadily in that position by the nurse or other female attendant. Sit down upon the bed just behind the patient, and introduce the middle finger of the left hand into the vagina as far as the recto-vaginal septum, and close the lips of the wound together over that finger with the forefinger and thumb of the same hand. Not more than two or at most three sutures will be required, unless the sphincter ani be torn through. The first suture should be made just in front of the anus. The needle should be passed from below upwards, through both lips of the wound, and through the whole thickness of the perineum; it should pierce the skin at a distance of at least a quarter of an inch from the edges of the wound. Care should be taken not to tie or twist the sutures too tightly, otherwise they are apt to cut out. The sutures should be removed at the end of a week.

Should the lacerated perineum not unite by the first intention, a surgical operation will, in all probability, be ultimately required to effect reunion. Most of the surgical operations for the cure of lacerated perineum consist in paring the edges of the wound, and bringing them together by sutures of various kinds.

Prolapsus Uteri—Treatment.

74. Prolapsus uteri, or "falling down of the womb," is a very common complaint amongst the poor. It

nearly always arises from getting up too soon after delivery, before the parts have had time to recover themselves. When it happens within the month, the woman should be kept in bed two or three weeks longer than usual, and (if the lochia have ceased) should use astringent injections.

There are various degrees of prolapsus uteri, from the slightest subsidence within the pelvis, to a complete appearance of the organ externally.

Prolapsus uteri is usually occasioned by some bearing-down effort within a few days after delivery, when the uterus is large and heavy, and all the parts which surround it and keep it in its place are relaxed and unable to support its weight. It is not at all uncommon to find poor women on the third day after delivery sitting up, and even attending to their household affairs. Hence the frequency of prolapsus uteri is not to be wondered at.

Women who have previously suffered from prolapsus uteri have sometimes been cured by remaining in bed two or three months after their confinement.

Injections of tannin, oak-bark, alum, sulphate of zinc, &c., may be used for the treatment of prolapsus.

There is some danger in using astringents before the lochia have ceased, because uterine inflammation might be produced by suddenly checking that discharge.

Paralysis of Legs after Delivery—Treatment.

75. Paralysis of one or both legs is sometimes met with after labour, and is caused by pressure on the sacral nerves during the second stage. There is a loss of power, and, frequently also, pain and numbness in the affected limb. These symptoms usually subside after three or four days, but in some instances last

much longer. Warm fomentations to the parts may be used, and also frictions with stimulating liniments.

The following liniment is a suitable one for such cases :—
  ℞ Liq. Ammon. Fortior, ʒj.
   Ol. Olivæ, ʒiss.
   Ol. Terebinth., ʒss.
   M. ft. liniment. ter die utend.

This kind of paralysis is a purely local affection, arising from the same cause as cramps during labour. (See 46, Part II.)

How to get rid of Secretion of Milk.

76. Women who have lost their infants, or who from any cause are prevented from nursing, are apt to suffer much inconvenience from accumulation of milk in the breasts. You must therefore take means to relieve the distended breasts, and also to get rid of the secretion of milk. For this purpose, a spare dry diet should be enjoined. The bowels should be moved every other day by laxatives, such as castor-oil, &c. Saline diaphoretics and diuretics may also be given. The breasts should be rubbed with warm oil, or covered with soap plasters spread on leather. If they are much distended, they should be rubbed with belladonna ointment, and a little milk should be drawn off by means of a syringe or breast-pump, taking care to abstract only just so much as is necessary to relieve tension.

The following mixture may be given :—
  ℞ Vin. Antimonial.,
   Spt. Æth. Nit., āā ʒij.
   Liq. Ammon. Acet., ʒj.
   Aq. Camph. ad ʒviij.
   M. Capt. sextam partem ter die.

Belladonna appears almost to have a specific effect in checking the secretion of milk, and relieving tension of the breast. The extract of belladonna should be mixed with an equal quantity of glycerine, and applied in a circle around the areola every night. This should be covered with two or three layers of lint or linen rag.

It has been found that iodide of potassium, in 20 or 25 grain doses, two or three times a day, will arrest the secretion of milk.

The breasts should never be completely emptied of milk, as this would only stimulate them to increased secretion.

Retracted Nipples—Treatment.

77. In some women the nipples are retracted, and so short that the child cannot seize them. In consequence of this malformation, all its efforts to suck are useless. Retracted nipples should be drawn out by means of an air-pump immediately before putting the child to the breast; which ought to be done before they are much distended. The use of a nipple-shield will sometimes enable the child to get at the milk.

Retraction of the nipple is produced by various causes, amongst which may be mentioned pressure from articles of dress, such as stays, &c.

It may be caused also by inflammation set up by the absurd and mischievous practice of pulling and squeezing the nipples of newly-born female children in order to "break the nipple strings," as the phrase is among nurses.

In the absence of a breast-pump, nurses are in the habit of drawing the nipples by suction with the mouth, or through a tube made for the purpose.

An older and stronger child will sometimes succeed where a newly-born infant has failed.

There is a common substitute for an air-pump which will answer well enough in many cases. A decanter or soda-water bottle is filled with hot water; the bottle is then emptied, and the nipple immediately inserted into its mouth. As the air cools within the bottle, a vacuum is created, which causes the nipple to project into it.

Sore Nipples.

78. Sore nipples are a frequent and distressing result of repeated applications of the child to the breasts. The soreness depends upon the presence of excoriations, chaps, fissures, or even deep ulcers upon and around the nipple. These usually appear in a few days after delivery, and, if severe, cause great pain, and sometimes bleed freely during lactation.

The nipples are more likely to become excoriated when they are retracted, or when, from any other cause, the child has much difficulty in seizing them.

A thin, tender skin, and a want of sebaceous secretion, will both predispose the nipples to excoriation.

Soreness of the nipples is sometimes caused by an aphthous condition of the child's mouth.

Sore Nipples—Treatment.

79. You may treat simple excoriations of the nipples by painting them with tincture of catechu or glycerinum acidi tannici, or washing them with weak lotions of alum or sulphate of zinc. If the excoriations are limited to the base of the nipple or its areola, you may cover them with a thin layer of collodion. But if there are deep fissures or ulcers, no application is so good as a solution of nitrate of silver. In all severe cases, the nipple should be protected during suckling by means of a proper shield.

The tincture of catechu should be undiluted; it may be applied once or twice a day by means of a camel's-hair brush.

The lotions of alum and sulphate of zinc may be of the strength of ℈j. to ℥vj. of water; that of the nitrate of silver, gr. x. to ℥j. of rose-water. These may be used twice a day.

Dr. Playfair speaks very highly of a lotion composed of ℥ss. of sulphurous acid, ℥ss. of glycerin of tannin, and ℥j. of water.

Burnt alum and ung. hydrarg. nitratis may be applied in some cases.

As most of these applications may have an injurious effect upon the child, the nipples should be carefully washed before it is put to the breast.

Collodion should not be applied over the apex of the nipples, so as to obstruct the milk-ducts.

Nipple-shields are of various kinds, and are made of metal, wood, or glass, with a cow's teat adapted to them, or an artificial teat consisting of wash-leather or india-rubber. In women who have suffered from sore nipples after previous confinements, it is a good plan to harden the skin of the nipples beforehand by washing them once a day with brandy and water, or painting them every other day with tincture of catechu.

Inflammation of Breasts—Symptoms.

80. The engorgement which accompanies the first flow of milk predisposes the breast to inflammation, and this is easily excited by any sudden exposure to cold or mental emotion. Inflammation also may extend to the breast from a sore nipple. The inflammation is phlegmonous in its character. There is local pain, soreness, redness, and circumscribed hardness. It is accompanied with shivering, febrile excitement, and temporary suspension of the secretion of milk. It may terminate in resolution or in suppuration.

The inflammation may involve only one or two lobules, and be comparatively superficial, or it may affect the whole breast and be deep-seated. In the latter case, there is much fever and a considerable elevation of the temperature, which may rise to 103° or 104° Fahr. The axillary glands are then hard and painful. When suppuration sets in, the inflamed part softens in the centre, the skin becomes thin, and the pus, after a few days, escapes. The abscess usually points near the nipple; but in persons of bad constitution the matter may be deep-seated, and may burrow extensively beneath the glandular structure of the breast. After a long time the abscess gives way, and a quantity of matter escapes, together with curdled milk and sloughs. Such cases, if left to themselves, are extremely tedious; troublesome sinuses are formed, which occasion great impairment of the general health.

In all cases the discharge of matter is considerable, and is accompanied for a time with night sweats and other hectic symptoms.

The suppuration not unfrequently occasions so much induration of the breast affected as to destroy its future use.

Inflammation of Breasts—Treatment.

81. Inflammation of the breast should be treated at its commencement by the application of ten or fifteen leeches to the part affected; or, if there be much fever, by general bleeding. The whole breast should then be covered with a soft linseed-meal poultice. Saline purgatives should be given, together with tartar-emetic diaphoretics. If the inflammation go on to suppuration, you should let out the matter with the lancet, as soon as you can detect fluctuation. In all these cases, however, you had better request a consultation.

A draught of sulphate of magnesia and infusion of senna is the best purgative to administer. Tartar-emetic may be given in ½-grain doses, with two or three grains of nitrate of potash.

When the matter is deep-seated, some tact is required, both to detect it and let it out. Care should be taken not to cut across the milk-ducts in so doing. If sinuses form, they must be laid open ; or if they run too deeply, they must be treated by stimulant injections, and pressure with straps of adhesive plaster. To effect this last object properly, the straps of plaster should be so arranged as to make firm and equable pressure over the whole breast, every part of which should be thus covered except the wound by which the matter has been evacuated.

In all cases of inflammation of the breast, there is a troublesome feeling of weight and dragging. This may be much relieved by supporting the breast with a sling placed round the neck.

Milk Fever—Symptoms.

82. The congestion and excitement of the mammary glands after labour may give rise to a certain amount of sympathetic fever. This is called "milk fever," and generally sets in on the third day, with shivering pain in the back and limbs, headache, quick full pulse, furred tongue, and feverishness, followed by profuse sweats, after which the febrile excitement subsides. The breasts are swollen, hard, and painful. There is an absence of abdominal tenderness, and a copious secretion of milk—two features which distinguish this complaint from more dangerous fevers.

When the fever is at its height there is sometimes slight delirium.

Milk fever is, *cæteris paribus*, more common in primiparæ than in multiparæ, and is much more likely to happen when the application of the child to the breast has been deferred too long.

Treatment of Milk Fever.

83. In the treatment of milk fever the patient should be kept on low diet, and should take aperients and saline diaphoretics. The ordinary dose of castor-oil may be somewhat increased, and repeated if necessary. The distended breasts must be relieved by early and frequent applications of the child, or, if necessary, by the breast-pump.

The following mixture may be given:—

℞ Vin. Ipecac.,
   Spt. Æth. Nit., āā ʒj.
   Sodæ et Potassæ Tart., ʒj.
   Aq. Camph. ad ʒviij.
   M. ft. mist. cujus sumat sextam partem ter die.

Ephemeral Fever.

84. Women, after delivery, are liable to a transitory fever, which has been named ephemeral fever, or (by the Germans) *Weid*. It may be brought on by fatigue, exposure to cold, or indigestion. Like an intermittent, it has a cold, a hot, and a sweating stage. The first is characterized by shivering, headache, and pains in the back and limbs; the second, by quick pulse, furred tongue, and fever; and the third, by profuse sweats and cessation of fever. The whole attack seldom exceeds twenty-four, or at most forty-eight hours. The bowels are usually costive, and the milk and lochia diminished or temporarily suspended.

This complaint is distinguished from puerperal fever by its paroxysmal character, and by the absence of marked abdominal tenderness.

Ephemeral fever most commonly attacks those whose health is somewhat impaired by a residence in low marshy districts.

Ephemeral Fever—Treatment.

85. During the cold stage of ephemeral fever, warmth should be applied to the surface, and warm drinks administered. During the hot stage, diaphoretics, such as Dover's powder, are indicated; and also smart purges of salts and senna. An emetic of gr. v. of ipecacuanha, at this stage, will sometimes serve to cut short the attack. After the fever is over, quinine should be given, especially if the attack seems at all likely to recur.

Miliary Fever.

86. Miliary fever is another affection occasionally met with after delivery. It is characterized by an eruption of very fine vesicles, about the size of a millet seed, and densely crowded together. It comes on two or three days after labour, with rigors, followed by fever and profuse perspiration. There is much headache, and oppression at the præcordia. The tongue is furred, with the papillæ red and prominent. The lochial discharge and milk are scanty. After a time the eruption comes out, having been preceded by tingling of the skin and copious perspirations. It

subsides after two or three days. This fever is distinguished from others by the peculiar eruption.

As the eruption recedes, the vesicles dry up, and the cuticle falls off in branny scales.

Miliary fever is most frequently met with in patients who have been kept in close, ill-ventilated rooms, with a large fire, and too much bed-clothing upon them.

Miliary Fever—Treatment.

87. Ventilation is of great importance in the treatment of miliary fever. The room should be kept cool, and some of the bed-clothes removed; at the same time, every care must be taken to avoid sudden exposure to cold. Cooling aperients should be given, and afterwards tonics and astringents.

The following aperient is a suitable one:—

  ℞ Magnes. Sulph., ℥ss.
   Infus. Rosæ Acid., ℥vj.
  M. Capt. sext. part. sextâ quâque horâ.

As a tonic the following mixture:—

  ℞ Tinct. Cinchonæ Co., ℥iij.
   Acid. Sulph. Arom., ℥ss.
   Aquam ad ℥vj.
  M. Capt. sext. part. bis die.

Purulent Ophthalmia of Infants.

88. Ophthalmia neonatorum is an acute conjunctivitis affecting the eyes of newly-born children, and is generally due to direct inoculation with unhealthy vaginal secretion, especially in women suffering from gonorrhœa or gleet. It usually comes on about three days after birth, with swelling of the eyelids and a mucous dis-

charge from the eyes, which soon becomes purulent. If neglected, it may lead to sloughing of the cornea, and blindness of one or both eyes.

This disease is a frequent cause of blindness, especially amongst the children of the poor. It is, therefore, of great importance that the student should at once be able to recognize and treat it.

Purulent Ophthalmia—Treatment.

89. After carefully clearing away the purulent secretion from the eyes by a stream of tepid water, a solution of two grains of nitrate of silver to an ounce of distilled water should be dropped into them every four hours. The edges of the eyelids should be anointed with simple ointment, to prevent their agglutination.

If the disease be not attended to at once, the eyelids may become so swollen that it is almost impossible to uncover the eyeballs and to wash away the very abundant secretion of matter. Unless this be done properly, lotions are but little use. A small syringe may be used for the purpose of washing, and the lotion may then be dropped into the eyes by means of a quill or camel's-hair brush.

The prophylactic treatment consists in carefully carrying out the rules of antiseptic midwifery; as follows:

Antiseptic Midwifery.

90. When there is reason to apprehend infection of any kind, antiseptic midwifery should be adopted. You should take with you some carbolic acid and a Higginson's syringe with elastic tube. The genital canal of the lying-in woman, as well as your hand that

is about to examine it, must be thoroughly disinfected. For this purpose a basin should first be filled with a two per cent. solution of carbolic acid in tepid water. After the external genitals of the woman and your hands and arms have been thoroughly cleansed with soap and water, the vagina should be well irrigated by an injection of the carbolic solution, and the hand and arm well bathed in the same fluid before making an examination. The same vaginal injection should be repeated afterwards.

The excellent results that have recently been obtained in the best regulated lying-in hospitals are due quite as much to the extreme cleanliness which is enjoined, as to the strict antiseptic precautions which are carried out in those institutions. In poor squalid dwellings, situated, perhaps, in some fœtid court or alley, where students often have to attend, it is almost impossible to enforce cleanliness, and very difficult to carry out antiseptic precautions thoroughly.

PART III.

CASES IN WHICH THE STUDENT OUGHT TO SEND FOR ASSISTANCE.

Abortion—Non-expulsion of the entire Ovum.

1. WHEN abortion has taken place, and the placenta, or any other portion of the ovum, remains behind in the uterus, give ergot, and make cautious attempts to bring it away with the finger. If you do not succeed, send for assistance.

These attempts will be rendered more easy if the uterus be previously depressed by means of the other hand placed above the pubis.

When the remainder of the ovum cannot be removed in the way just mentioned, the case is one of some difficulty, and requires delicacy of manipulation. The introduction of the hand, or of some instrument for the purpose, will probably be necessary. If the placenta is allowed to remain in the uterus it may cause secondary hæmorrhage (See 70, Part II.), or decompose and produce septicæmia from absorption of putrid matter.

Abortion with Profuse Hæmorrhage.

2. In cases of abortion, accompanied with profuse

hæmorrhage, before sending, apply cold, as directed in 57, Part II. Give a full dose of ergot, and plug the vagina.

A hæmorrhage is profuse when it produces marked constitutional symptoms, such as those described in 55, Part II. Cases of miscarriage, under such circumstances, are attended with considerable risk.

The plug or "tampon" is a powerful means of arresting hæmorrhage in certain conditions of the uterus. By its presence it stimulates that organ to contraction, and also exerts a pressure upon the bleeding vessels. As a general rule, the plug should not be used, under the circumstances above mentioned, after the period of quickening. Before that period, the uterus is incapable of containing any large amount of blood; but after that time there would be considerable danger of internal hæmorrhage.

For the purpose of plugging the vagina, a tolerably large sponge may be used, or a soft silk or cambric handkerchief. This should be well oiled and introduced into the vagina, beginning with one of the corners. There is, however, nothing so good for this purpose as antiseptic cotton wool. This should be made into a number of pledgets, to each of which a string is attached to facilitate withdrawal.

If a large speculum is at hand, the plug may be introduced through it with much more ease and much less discomfort to the patient. The plug is much less apt to become offensive if previously anointed with carbolized oil or glycerine. But, under any circumstances, it is not well to leave it in the vagina more than twelve hours, because the retained blood and discharges putrefy and become a source of irritation.

Extra-uterine Fœtation—Rupture of the Cyst.

3. In cases of suspected extra-uterine fœtation, when certain symptoms set in which indicate a rupture of the cyst. These are—sudden and acute pain in one

iliac region, followed by great exhaustion, vomiting, and symptoms of internal hæmorrhage. Before sending, place the patient in the horizontal posture, apply a binder round the abdomen, and cold, by means of a bladder containing ice, to the part. If there is severe collapse, give stimulants.

In extra-uterine fœtation the impregnated ovum, from some cause or other, does not reach the uterus, but is developed externally to it, either in the ovary, the Fallopian tube, or in the walls of the uterus. This curious freak of nature is by no means of common occurrence. The diagnosis is very uncertain; most of the signs of pregnancy are present, but the tumour formed by the impregnated ovum presents itself on one side of the abdomen, usually the iliac fossa. Pain is frequently felt in that region, accompanied with vomiting. The menses, in most cases, continue during extra-uterine gestation. After a variable time, the cyst containing the ovum gives way, and the woman dies from the sudden shock to the system, and profuse internal hæmorrhage thus occasioned. Such is the usual history of these cases. The cyst is generally ruptured during the first half of gestation. But there are many instances on record of women who have survived both the shock and subsequent inflammation, and in whom the fœtus has been evacuated by abscess, or retained for months, and even years.

As a last resource, "laparotomy" has been performed. This operation consists in opening the abdominal cavity by an incision, and removing the entire cyst and tube after tying the pedicle as in ovariotomy. All effused blood and clots must be removed by carbolized sponges, and every other antiseptic precaution adopted.

Expulsion of Moles, attended with much Hæmorrhage.

4. In cases of mole pregnancy, when the expulsion of the mole is attended with much hæmorrhage, and when portions of it remain behind in the uterus. In

these cases, as in an abortion, you may give ergot, apply cold, and use the plug, before sending for assistance.

Moles are shapeless masses, which are, properly speaking, the result of conception, and consist of various degenerations of the ovum. In many of them scarcely any portion of the ovum can be traced, the mass consisting of semi-organized coagula and layers of fibrine. This is the fleshy mole. In others, the fœtal coverings, especially the chorion, have become developed into innumerable vesicles, resembling bunches of grapes or currants. This is the hydatid mole. When the uterus contains a mole, the earlier signs of pregnancy present themselves; but the latter signs, such as the "ballottement," the fœtal movements, and the sounds of the fœtal heart, are wanting. After an uncertain period, the uterus expels the mole, with all the symptoms of an abortion. The expulsion of the hydatid mole is attended with most risk; it is usually accompanied with much hæmorrhage, and the mole frequently does not come away entire. When this happens, the introduction of the hand may become necessary.

Retroversion of the Gravid Uterus.

5. This dangerous displacement may occur during the first four months of pregnancy, and is usually the result of accident. It is caused by some sudden or violent effort, especially when the bladder happens to be very full. The fundus uteri is forced backwards and downwards beneath the sacral promontory, and the os tilted forwards and upwards against the symphysis pubis (Fig. 13). The pressure thus produced on the bladder and rectum gives rise to retention of urine and other urgent symptoms, which, if not soon relieved, may ultimately prove fatal.

Pregnancy sometimes occurs in a uterus already retroverted, but when such is the case, the unfavourable symptoms are developed much more gradually. After the uterus has risen out of the pelvis, retroversion is almost impossible. If unrelieved, retroversion may cause rupture of the bladder, peritonitis, inflammation, and sloughing of the bladder and uterus, &c., any of which results may prove fatal.

FIG. 13.

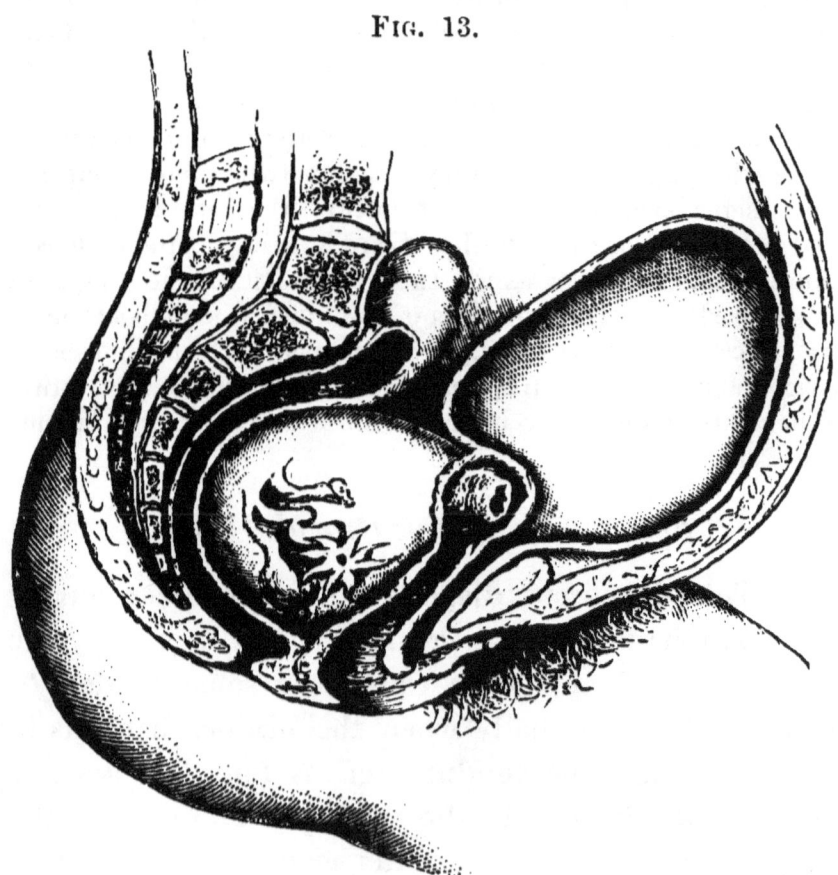

Diagnosis of Retroversion.

6. The sudden occurrence of bearing-down pain with retention of urine, ought to excite suspicion; and

this ought to lead to an examination by vagina and rectum. The hollow of the sacrum will then be found to be filled with a firm globular mass, which presses down low between the vagina and rectum. The vagina will be felt running directly upwards behind the symphysis pubis, whilst the os uteri will be so high as to be almost out of reach.

The abdomen is generally enlarged and painful to the touch, in consequence of great distension of the bladder. The meatus urinarius is sometimes drawn up into the vagina and nearly obliterated.

Treatment of Retroversion.

7. The distended bladder should be at once relieved. Having sent the patient to bed, you draw off the urine with an elastic male catheter, and, if necessary, empty the rectum by an enema. The next step is to replace the uterus. But as this is sometimes a difficult operation, and as it may be delayed for a time with safety, it will be better to send for assistance.

The urethra is so much elongated, compressed, and drawn up out of its usual course, that it is absolutely necessary to use a long elastic catheter.

The following mode of replacing the uterus has been found by the author to be the most satisfactory :—Having placed the patient on her elbows and knees, so as to invert the pelvis, the forefinger of one hand is passed into the vagina, and the middle finger of the same hand into the rectum. The fundus uteri is then pressed steadily upwards until it passes above the sacral promontory.

Should the reduction be very difficult, the patient should first inhale chloroform.

Should it be found impossible to effect reduction, it will be necessary to lessen the bulk of the uterus by puncturing the membranes and bringing on abortion.

In some cases, where the os uteri could not be reached, the fundus uteri has been punctured by a trochar from the vagina with a successful result.

Symptoms of Powerless Labour.

8. In any case of difficult labour, or otherwise, when symptoms of powerless labour *begin* to show themselves. These are—diminished frequency and force of the pains, considerable acceleration of the pulse between the pains, increased temperature, severe rigors and vomiting, restlessness, dry furred tongue, retention of urine, heat and tenderness of the vagina, with brownish and occasionally fœtid discharge.

Powerless labour is always the result of a prolonged second stage, whether it be from obstruction of the head, or from inefficient uterine efforts. There is no precise period at which the unfavourable symptoms set in, but in general they are likely to do so after the second stage has lasted twelve hours. No prudent practitioner would allow such symptoms to become developed; but, taking alarm at their first onset, would proceed to assist nature by art.

The pains in powerless labour lose the forcing character of the second stage, and bear no resemblance to those of the first. The pulse may range from 100 to 130, or even to 140, between the pains.

If the above symptoms are allowed to continue unrelieved, the condition of the patient becomes much worse; the tongue is dry and brown, sordes collect about the teeth, the pulse is very rapid and weak; the matter ejected by vomiting is dark, sometimes consisting of grumous blood; the abdomen becomes tense and tender, the surface cold and clammy; the restlessness passes on to jactitation, delirium, and death.

Minute or Imperforate Os Uteri.

9. When labour is obstructed by a minute or imperforate os uteri, which is the result of structural change, and which does not yield to time and the usual remedies for an undilatable os uteri. (See 12, Part II.)

This condition of the os uteri may be caused by cicatrices resulting from mechanical injuries, by inflammation, or by scirrhous deposit in the part. In some cases, there is complete agglutination of the os uteri. The inferior portion of the uterus becomes very tense, and is forced down low into the pelvis with each pain; but the finger, in examining, can detect merely a depression, and no opening in the part. In some rare instances, a circular portion of the inferior part of the uterus has yielded to the force of the pains, and separated, so as to allow the child to pass. In others, it has been necessary to make a crucial incision in the part before delivery could be accomplished.

Strictures of Vagina.

10. When labour is obstructed by strictures of the vaginal canal, produced by structural alterations, such as cicatrices, callosities, adhesions, &c., which do not yield to time and the usual remedies for rigidity of the soft parts. (See 18. Part II.)

These structural lesions of the vagina are nearly always the result of sloughing and loss of substance, produced by a previous hard labour. The cicatrices may form rings, or spirals, around various parts of the vagina, or there may be a partial or complete occlusion of some part of the canal. The cicatrices are sometimes gristly and semi-cartilaginous. It may be necessary to divide them with the knife, or even to lessen the size of the child's head by craniotomy. Such operations, of course, require a consultation.

Obstructed Labour from Pelvic Tumours.

11. When labour is obstructed by tumours of various kinds within the pelvis, and the difficulty appears to be insuperable by the natural efforts.

The tumours may be either within or without the vagina, and may grow from the mucous membrane of the uterus and vagina, or from the exterior of the uterus, its appendages, or other contents of the pelvis. When these tumours are outside the vagina, they are usually met with in the cul-de-sac of the peritoneum between the vagina and rectum, where they produce a bulging of the posterior wall of the vagina. The tumours may be solid growths, such as polypi, fibrous, fatty, sarcomatous, and scirrhous masses, or cysts containing fluid, such as ovarian tumours, &c. Sometimes a hernia descends into the vagina during labour. The intestine comes down into the cul-de-sac between the vagina and rectum, and forms a tumour, covered by the posterior wall of the vagina. In some rare instances the bladder contains a calculus, which descends before the head during labour. The tumour thus formed is covered by the upper wall of the vagina like a vaginal cystocele, but is firm and hard, and not soft and fluctuating.

The chief danger from calculus is not so much from the obstacle which it presents, as from the injury which it may inflict upon the bladder, when it becomes compressed between the head and the pubis. In most cases it is possible to push the calculus above the pelvic brim; but if this should be impracticable, vaginal lithotomy may be necessary. In short, in all cases of pelvic tumours, the treatment must depend very much on the circumstances of the case: some tumours are movable, and may be pushed above the head; others, such as polypi, &c., admit of excision; others, such as ovarian tumours, may be tapped. All these operations, except the first, are attended with risk, and require much judgment. If any such operation be impracticable, delivery with the forceps, or craniotomy, may be required.

Prolapse of Bladder during Labour.

12. When there is a prolapse of the bladder during labour. In such cases the bladder descends before the head, and forms a fluctuating tumour, covered by the upper wall of the vagina. The finger readily passes beneath and behind the tumour, until it reaches the head. Before sending, evacuate the bladder, if possible, by passing a gum-elastic catheter with the point directed downwards and backwards.

Prolapse of the bladder, or vaginal cystocele, is a rare complaint. It is occasioned by relaxation of the upper wall of the vagina, and other connections of the bladder. The symptoms are—fulness, tension, and dragging, with a constant desire to pass water, and much difficulty in doing so. If there has been complete retention of urine for some time, there is considerable risk that the pressure of the head may cause a rupture of the bladder.

Difficult Labour from Pelvic Deformity — Diagnosis.

13. When labour is obstructed in the second stage by pelvic deformity. In these cases, the head is arrested in its progress at some particular part of the pelvis (generally the brim), and remains immovable, notwithstanding there may have been strong forcing pains for some hours. The scalp becomes very tumid, and the bones overlap very much, so as to give the vertex a conical shape. You need not be in a hurry to send for assistance in such cases (See 44, Part II.); but you must do so without delay if there be the least symptom of powerless labour, or if the head

become impacted, *i.e.*, so firmly fixed that it cannot recede between the pains, and can only be displaced with great difficulty.

Deformities of the pelvis are occasioned by rickets during childhood, mollities ossium in adult age, bony growths, fractures, &c. The deformity may affect the brim, cavity, or outlet of the pelvis. The brim is most usually affected, and the most ordinary kind of deformity is a prominent sacrum, causing a diminution of the antero-posterior diameter of the brim. The pelvis in such case becomes heart-shaped.

The degree of deformity may vary very much, but it is most readily estimated by measuring the antero-posterior diameter of the brim. This may be done by introducing the tips of four fingers of one hand in a line between the sacral promontory and pubis. If they cannot be separated, for instance, there is much deformity; but if they can be separated widely there is little or none. Again, if the forefinger, during an ordinary examination, impinges on the upper part of the sacrum, we have reason to believe that the deformity is considerable.

The existence of pelvic deformity may also be ascertained by the great difficulty which is experienced in passing up the forefinger between the head and the different parts of the pelvis. Distortions of the cavity and outlet of the pelvis are not so common; they generally depend on unnatural straightness of the sacrum, approximation of the tubera ischii, narrowing of the pubic arch, or anchylosis of the coccyx, &c. They produce much the same symptoms as distortions of the brim, except that they arise at a later period of the labour.

The symptoms occasioned by deformity of the brim have been very accurately described by Dr. Rigby. "Besides the general appearance of the patient," he says, "we frequently find that the uterine contractions are very irregular; that they have but little effect in dilating the os uteri; the head does not descend against it, but remains high up; it shows no disposition to enter the pelvic cavity, and rests upon the symphysis pubis, against which it presses very forcibly, being pushed forward by the promontory of the sacrum." When the deformity is not very considerable, it often happens that, after some hours of severe pain, the difficulty is suddenly overcome, the head passes, and the rest of the labour is speedily accomplished.

When, however, the deformity is more considerable, the forceps is likely to be required; when it is still greater, the accoucheur is reduced to the painful necessity of destroying the child by craniotomy. Again, where the distortion is extreme, delivery *per vias naturales* becomes impossible. The Cæsarean section is then the last resource of art.

The forceps is inadmissible when the antero-posterior diameter of the pelvis is less than three inches; because it has been laid down as a rule, that a living child cannot pass through a pelvis of such dimensions. Craniotomy, or the cephalotribe, may be employed when the antero-posterior diameter is not more than three inches, or less than an inch and a half. When it is less than an inch and a half, delivery *per vias naturales* is scarcely possible.

Impaction of the head is always attended with considerable danger. The constant and severe pressure upon the soft parts lining the pelvis will almost certainly produce inflammation and sloughing of those parts. Hence there is a necessity for prompt interference.

Arrest of Head in Cavity of Pelvis.

14. When the head is arrested, either in the cavity or outlet of the pelvis, in consequence of some want of power in the uterus, and also some slight disproportion between the head and pelvis. The time when you ought to send must depend very much upon the state of the patient; but, as a general rule, you ought to do so before the head has been arrested as long as four hours.

In the preceding case the use of the forceps is indicated.

Ergot of rye is inadmissible, because there is a mechanical obstacle to the delivery, as well as a want of power.

Unless the condition of the patient be such as to require interference, the forceps should not be used whilst the pains continue regular, and the head advances ever so little.

Cases in which no Presentation can be felt.

15. In the first stage of labour, when the os uteri is dilated to the size of a crown piece, or even larger, and no presentation can be detected, although you have made a careful examination with both hands.

When no presentation can be felt, although the os uteri is widely dilated, there is in all probability what nurses call a "cross-birth," *i.e.*, the long axis of the child is at right angles with the axis of the pelvis, the shoulder or arm presenting.

When the child is in this position, the presentation seldom descends sufficiently low to be felt at any early period of the labour. In such cases the greatest care is necessary in examining, lest the membranes be ruptured; because, as turning will in all probability be required, the escape of the liquor amnii would render that operation very difficult.

The presentation may also remain out of reach in a similar manner when the pelvis is deformed, or the child's head hydrocephalic.

Cases of Brow Presentation.

16. In cases of brow presentation. These unfavourable presentations of the head are recognized by the facility with which you can reach the great fontanelle and also the upper part of the face, the one being turned towards one side of the pelvis, and the other

towards the opposite side, the presenting part being one of the frontal eminences. (*Fig.* 15.)

FIG. 14.

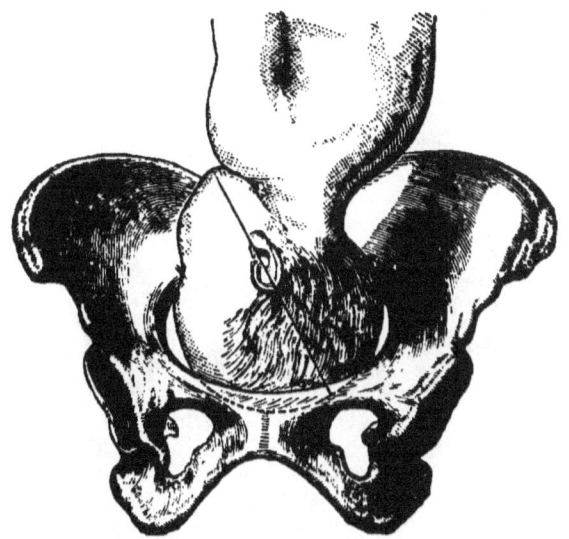

Presentations of the brow are intermediate between those

FIG. 15.

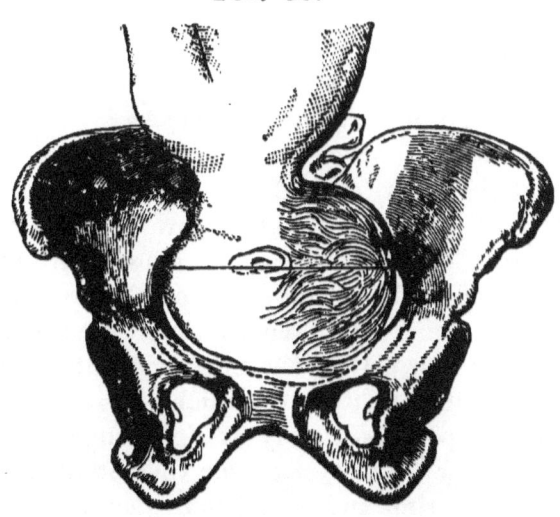

of the vertex and those of the face, approaching, however,

more nearly to the latter than to the former. When the vertex presents, the head is said to be flexed upon the body, so that the chin is close to the chest (*Fig.* 14); when the face presents, the head is extended completely, and the chin is as far removed from the chest as the neck will admit of (*Fig.* 16).

FIG. 16.

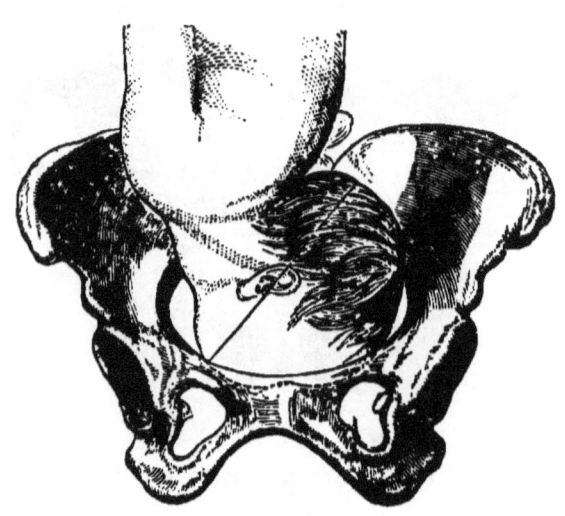

In a brow presentation the head is partially extended, so that one of the frontal bones presents, most commonly either the right or left frontal eminence (*Fig.* 15). At the commencement of labour the presenting part may be included in a circle, the circumference of which touches the root of the nose on one side, and the great fontanelle on the other. On examining at this stage of the labour, the face would be found usually looking towards one sacro-iliac synchondrosis, and the great fontanelle towards the acetabulum of the opposite side, or *vice versâ*. As the head descends lower, and becomes more fully engaged in the pelvis, the mento-occipital diameter will correspond with one of the oblique diameters of the pelvis, and thus will take a position nearly at right angles to that which it occupies in an ordinary case; for then it is parallel to the axis of the pelvic brim, and is perpendicular to these diameters. In a brow presentation the head is placed in the most unfavourable manner possible for traversing the brim of the pelvis; for the longest diameter of the head (the occipito-mental, which measures five inches) corresponds with the oblique diameter of the pelvic brim, measuring only four inches and a half. It is, therefore, scarcely possible for the head to traverse the pelvis in this position; and it will be found, as a general rule, that manual interference is necessary in the treatment of these cases. The forehead may be pushed up, or the chin brought down, so as to convert it into either a vertex or face presentation. Any attempts to effect the first will probably prove unsuccessful, but the last may readily be accomplished either by the fingers or the vectis.

Arrest of Child's Body in Breech Presentations.

17. In breech presentation, when the breech is arrested in the cavity of the pelvis, from want of room or from insufficient uterine action.

The rules which are applicable in cases of arrest of the head (See 14, Part III.), respecting the time to send for assistance, will also apply to breech cases. When the breech is arrested, it may be necessary to assist the delivery. This is usually done by hooking the finger over the groin, and making traction in concert with the pains. Some recommend a blunt hook for this purpose, whilst others advise the use of the forceps. Without much care, the first of these instruments would be likely to inflict injury on the child; and the same may be said of the second, which is indeed scarcely suitable for breech cases. This objection does not apply to the use of a fillet, such as that recommended by the author in the *Obstetrical Transactions,* vol. xvii. Dr. Barnes advises that in these cases a foot should be brought down.

Arrest of Head in Breech Presentations.

18. In breech presentations, when the head is arrested at the brim of the pelvis, and cannot be

brought through by rectifying its position and making cautious and steady traction on the neck.

In these cases there is generally some want of room in the pelvic brim. The forceps has been recommended, but its utility is very questionable. The child is almost sure to be dead from pressure on the cord, and the best plan then is to lessen the size of the head by opening it behind the ear, and evacuating the brain.

Presentations of Superior Extremities—Diagnosis.

19. In presentations of the superior extremity, *i.e.*,

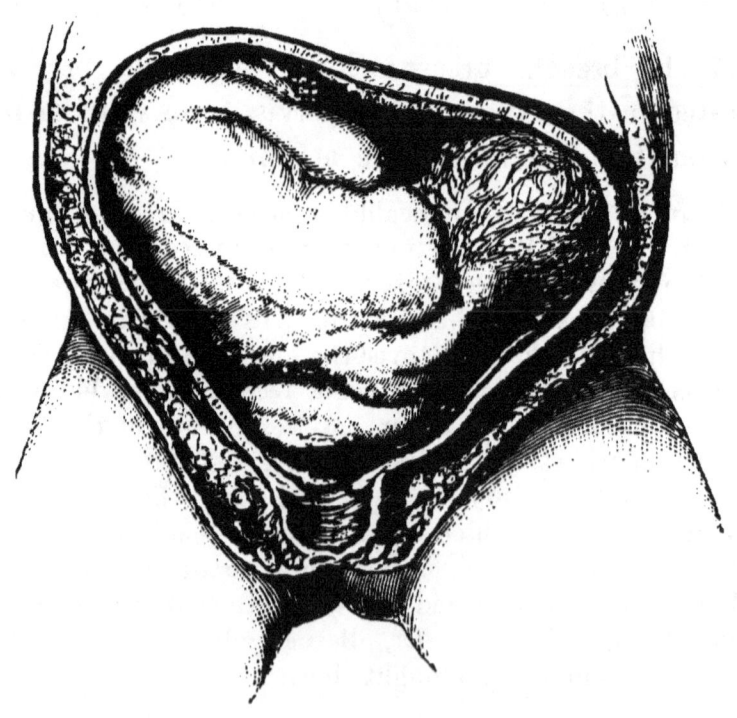

FIG. 17.

either the shoulder, elbow, or hand. These occur about once in 231 cases. The shoulder is known by its being more pointed than either the head or the breech. You recognize it by feeling the clavicle and spine and acromion process of the scapula; and, above all, by the ribs, which will at once distinguish it from any other part of the body. (For characteristics of the elbow, see 33, Part II.; and of the hand, see 32, Part II.)

When the superior extremities present, the child is placed transversely with regard to the pelvis. (*Fig.* 17.) Delivery in this position is almost impossible, but still may take place in rare exceptional instances by a natural process of expulsion, to which the name "spontaneous evolution" has been given. Such an unusual occurrence should never be depended on in practice. The presentation should be altered by turning the child and bringing down the feet.

Assistance should be sent for immediately, as soon as a presentation of the superior extremities is detected. Too much care cannot be taken lest the membrane be ruptured by injudicious examinations.

In shoulder presentations the hand and arm usually prolapse after the rupture of the membranes, and remove all doubt, if any existed before, as to the nature of the presentation.

Monsters.

20. When labour is obstructed, in consequence of abnormal development or monstrosity of the foetus.

Extraordinary size of the foetus, or unusual ossification of its head, may act as causes of difficult labour, and render the use of the forceps necessary.

Monsters are of two kinds, viz., monsters by deficiency and by excess. The former class will be puzzling as regards diagnosis, but present no difficulties as to delivery. The latter class, however, may occasion obstacles of a serious kind; in most cases, various parts of two (or more) children are united together. The treatment must depend very much upon the circumstances of each case. When there is much difficulty, turning or embryotomy may be required; or, perhaps, both these operations.

Hydrocephalus or Ascites of Fœtus—Diagnosis.

21. When labour is obstructed, in consequence of increased size of the child's head from hydrocephalus, or of its abdomen from ascites. Hydrocephalus is distinguished by the very large size of the head, which occupies the entire contour of the superior strait of the pelvis; and a bimanual examination is the surest mode of recognizing this. The head is resisting during a contraction, and soft and fluctuating in the intervals of pain. The sutures (especially the sagittal) and fontanelles are unusually open, and the cranial bones are widely separated from one another. Ascites is distinguished by the large size of the abdomen, and the distinct sense of fluctuation which it communicates to the finger.

In either of these cases, the increased size of the child's head or body may occasion a train of symptoms similar to those which arise in the course of a difficult labour, from diminished size of the pelvis.

When the bones are widely separated, the tips of the fingers may be passed between, and even slightly beneath them.

Hydrocephalic infants may be expelled by the natural powers, provided the pelvis is roomy; but the labour is usually very tedious and difficult. In most cases assistance will be required; the size of the head must be lessened by puncturing it with a small trocar in one of the sutures, and letting out the fluid. The abdomen may be tapped, in a similar way, in ascites.

Prolapse of Umbilical Cord—Diagnosis.

22. When there is a prolapse of the umbilical cord during labour. In this case (which happens about once in 221 labours), before the membranes rupture, you may feel through them a small, soft, movable body, which may be readily displaced, and has a rapid pulsation isochronous with the fœtal heart. After the membranes have ruptured, the diagnosis is very easy; for the cord can readily be felt in the vagina. Sometimes it is prolapsed beyond the os externum. As soon as you have ascertained the existence of this complication, you must send for assistance without delay, having previously placed the woman on her elbows and knees; but if you find that the cord is quite destitute of pulsation, you may let the labour take its course.

A prolapse of the funis does not make any difference in the course of a labour, as regards the mother; but it is a complication fraught with the utmost danger to the child. If a prolapsed cord cannot be reduced, the child will almost inevitably die before the termination of the labour, from pressure on the umbilical vessels. There are several causes which may produce this accident, such as unfavourable presentations, irregularity in the shape of the pelvis, sudden escape of a large quantity of liquor amnii, excessive length of cord,* low insertion of the cord into the placenta, or attachment of the placenta to the neck of the uterus, &c.

When the cord can be felt distinctly pulsating, some interference is necessary to save the life of the child, provided that the os uteri is sufficiently dilated to allow it. Various means have been devised for reducing the cord, and keeping it up out

---

* In a case occurring in the author's practice, the cord measured five feet in length.

of the way until the presenting part has descended and fully occupied the pelvic cavity. One of the best of these is the postural method just mentioned. In this position, on the elbows and knees, the cord naturally gravitates towards the fundus uteri. If these devices fail, turning will be necessary. If the labour be too far advanced for turning, the forceps may be used.

When the cord is cold and pulseless, the child is dead: there is, therefore, no necessity for interference.

Accidental Hæmorrhage—Diagnosis.

23. In cases of accidental hæmorrhage, *i.e.*, hæmorrhage arising before birth from a casual detachment of part of the placenta whilst in its normal situation. This hæmorrhage comes on shortly before or at the full term of pregnancy, and is generally the result of some sudden shock, either mental or bodily. It commences with dull pain and aching in the belly and back. The uterus feels firmer, tenser, and perceptibly larger than before. After a time, the usual symptoms of hæmorrhage supervene (See 55, Part II.), and, in most cases, fluid blood and coagula escape externally. The os uteri is soft and dilatable. If you pass your finger within it and around its circumference, you feel the smooth bag of the waters presenting. If labour pains are present, the hæmorrhage is arrested during the pains, but returns in the interval; whereas the exact converse takes place in unavoidable hæmorrhage.

The detachment of the placenta is mostly partial; but in some exceptional cases the placenta is wholly detached. Again, the hæmorrhage may be entirely internal, and concealed from observation. The hæmorrhage may be a result of general plethora, as well as of any sudden shock, such as coughing, sneezing, vomiting, over-exertion, blows, falls, &c.

When the os uteri is smooth and regular throughout its *entire* circumference, and the membranes can be felt presenting, we may be sure that the hæmorrhage is not occasioned by placenta prævia, especially if it cease during the pains. The hæmorrhage is arrested during a pain, because the bleeding vessels are compressed by the contracting fibres of the uterus.

Treatment of Accidental Hæmorrhage.

24. As soon as you have sent for assistance, you must take some means to check the hæmorrhage. If the term of pregnancy has not expired, if the hæmorrhage be not profuse, if there be no pains and little or no dilatation of the os uteri, place the woman in the recumbent posture, and let her be kept cool and quiet. Apply ice-bags or cold compresses to the abdomen and vulva, give cold drinks, and use enemata of cold water. Also administer astringents and sedatives. But if labour pains have set in, if the os uteri be dilated, and the hæmorrhage severe, you must use, in addition, measures which will increase uterine contraction, such as the administration of ergot and the application of the binder. If these fail, you may rupture the membranes.

If the term of pregnancy be not completed, we may hope, in some instances, to restrain the hæmorrhage, and conduct the woman safely to the full time.

The following mixture may be given :—

℞ Acid. Sulph. Dil., ʒss.
Tinct. Opii, ℳxl.
Infus. Rosæ Acid. ad ʒvj.

M. ft. mistura, cujus sumat sextam partem omni horâ

Or the following:—

> ℞ Plumbi Acetat., gr. xviij.
> Acid. Acetic., ♏xx.
> Morphiæ Acetat., gr. j.
> Aq. Destillat., ʒvj.
> M. Capt. sextam partem secundâ quâque horâ.

The plug has been much recommended in these cases; but it is a hazardous remedy, especially in the hands of an inexperienced practitioner.

Rupturing the membranes is one of the surest means both for restraining hæmorrhage and forwarding the labour. When the liquor amnii has escaped, the uterus contracts firmly around the body of the child, at the same time compressing the placenta, and closing the bleeding vessels. It should, however, only be adopted by the student as a last resource, because it may possibly fail, and the result would be that the operation of turning, which might be required, would be thus rendered difficult.

Placenta Prævia—Diagnosis.

25. In cases of unavoidable hæmorrhage. In these, the placenta is attached over or very near the os uteri; and the necessary result is, that, as soon as the os begins to open, the placenta becomes detached, and a copious hæmorrhage takes place. The flooding usually comes on a few weeks before delivery, and is at first inconsiderable. After a week or two it returns more copiously, until, at last, it becomes frequent and profuse. The flooding accompanies each uterine contraction, and ceases in the intervals between them. On examining, you either find that the entire os uteri is thickened, and occupied by the firm, rough, spongy mass of the placenta, or you find that the os is partly

occupied by the placenta and partly by the membranes. The first is a complete, and the second a partial, presentation of the placenta.

The hæmorrhage from placenta prævia is occasioned, first, by the slight dilatation of the cervix uteri which takes place some weeks before delivery; and, subsequently, by the still further dilatation which is effected during labour. The opening of the cervix produces a disruption of the connections between the placenta and uterus; the large venous sinuses of the latter are laid open, and frightful hæmorrhage ensues, which increases *pari passu* with the pains.

Placenta prævia is the most dangerous of all presentations. In a record of 21 cases of placenta prævia, published by the author,* the secondary danger of death from septicæmia is shown to be quite as great as the primary danger from hæmorrhage. If labour be permitted to go on under such circumstances without interference, the woman will almost certainly bleed to death before its termination. Still, however, a few exceptional cases occur in which nature effects delivery without a fatal result. In these the uterine contractions are very powerful and energetic. The placenta speedily becomes detached and expelled, and the hæmorrhage ceases. As soon as the placenta is completely detached, the uterine arteries are broken away from it, and the veins are closed by the dilatation of the os uteri which effected the separation, as well as by the direct compression of the child's head, which soon descends, and occupies the place of the placenta.

Placenta Prævia—Treatment.

26. In cases of placenta prævia, send immediately for assistance, and try to arrest the hæmorrhage by placing the woman in the recumbent posture, by cold applications to the abdomen and vulva, by cold drinks

---

* 'Bristol Medico-Chirurgical Journal," Dec., 1883.

and enemata, and by repeated doses of opium. If the full term has not yet arrived, these means may for a time succeed. If they should fail, you may plug the vagina until assistance arrives. If there is a partial placenta presentation, you may rupture the membranes, as in accidental hæmorrhage. In all cases, stimuli are to be given, if necessary.

In cases of complete placenta presentation, the proper treatment is to turn and deliver, as soon as the os uteri is sufficiently dilatable to allow of such a proceeding. When the diagnosis is clear, nearly all recent authorities are in favour of prompt interference on the first occurrence of hæmorrhage. As Dr. King truly remarks: "The child will seldom be saved by temporizing, and the mother often dies with the recurrence of hæmorrhage, the bleeding coming on suddenly, as it is apt to do, in the absence of the physician. The best rule is to *deliver as soon as practicable after the first occurrence of hæmorrhage, whether the child is viable or not.*" *

In some instances, where the exhaustion from hæmorrhage is very great, and when turning would be dangerous, complete detachment of the placenta has been recommended, and practised with success. (See Sir J. Simpson's memoirs on this subject.) Should the inferior extremities present with placenta prævia, it is a fortunate circumstance, because there will be no need of turning.

When the membranes have been ruptured in partial placenta prævia, the head descends, compresses the placenta and the bleeding vessels of the uterus, and thus stays the hæmorrhage.

Puerperal Convulsions: Epileptic Form—Symptoms.

27. In all cases of puerperal convulsions or eclampsia. These usually assume the form of epilepsy, and may supervene before, during, or after labour. They are

---

* King's "Manual of Obstetrics."

generally preceded by headache, drowsiness, obscure vision, and tinnitus aurium. As the fit comes on, the woman loses consciousness, the pupils become dilated, and the countenance rigid. All the muscles of the body are seized with violent spasmodic contractions; the face is livid and horribly distorted, the respiration hissing, the tongue is thrust out, and a bloody foam issues from the mouth. After a few minutes the fit passes off, and returns again in half an hour, an hour, or more. According to the severity of the case, consciousness may be completely, partially, or not at all, regained during the intervals.

The muscular contractions during the paroxysms are so violent, that the attendants often have the greatest difficulty in keeping the patient upon the bed. The tongue being thrust out, it is very liable to be bitten, in consequence of the contractions of the muscles of the jaw. Hence it is that the saliva is so apt to be tinged with blood. The urine and fæces are often expelled involuntarily during the convulsions. The progress of labour, although in some degree interfered with, is not arrested by the convulsions. The fits are apt to recur simultaneously with the pains, and the child may be born during one of these paroxysms. Under such circumstances it is very likely to be dead, or to die soon after its birth.

In bad cases the breathing remains stertorous, and the patient lies in a comatose state between the fits.

Epileptic convulsions may occur in very opposite conditions of the circulatory system. In most cases they appear to be connected with a state of hyperæmia. In some few instances they have been noticed in connection with extreme anæmia, from flooding. In by far the greater number a state of toxæmia has been recognized, by the presence of albumen in the urine. It must be obvious that diametrically opposite principles of treatment would apply to the first and second class of cases.

Hysterical and Apoplectic Convulsions—Diagnosis.

28. Besides the epileptic form of convulsions, there are the hysterical and apoplectic. These are distinguished from the first by the following marks :—The hysterical convulsions usually come on during the early months of pregnancy, and resemble ordinary hysterical paroxysms, being unaccompanied with complete loss of consciousness, distortion of the face, or foaming of the mouth. After the attack is over, the patient resumes her ordinary condition. Apoplectic convulsions mostly come on during the second stage of labour, and resemble a severe attack of apoplexy; the convulsion shows no disposition to return, and is speedily followed by stertorous breathing, and complete loss of thought, sensation, and voluntary motion, until, at last, all muscular action ceases.

Hysterical convulsions most commonly happen about the time of quickening. They require very different treatment from that which is needed in the other two kinds, and are of far less serious import.

Apoplectic convulsions are almost invariably fatal, and, in general, depend upon a sudden rupture of one of the cerebral vessels. In persons predisposed to apoplexy, the great stress upon the vessels of the brain during the second stage of labour is very likely to produce such a result.

Treatment of Convulsions.

29. In all cases of convulsions, send for assistance immediately. In the meantime you should take precautions to prevent the woman from injuring herself during the paroxysms. You should see that she does

not roll off the bed, and insert a cork or pad of some kind between the teeth, to prevent her from biting her tongue. The following remedies may be used in all cases, viz., cold affusion to the head, and sinapisms to the calves of the legs, together with purgatives and anti-spasmodic enemata.

The following enema may be mixed with a pint of warm water or thin gruel, and injected into the rectum:—

  R Ol. Terebinth.,
   Træ. Assafœtid., āā ℥ss.
   Ovi Vitellum,
   Ol. Ricini, ℥j. M.

The student should always request a consultation in all cases of puerperal convulsions, because a widely different treatment is required in the several forms of convulsions; hence an error in diagnosis might be attended with dangerous or even fatal results. For instance, in the epileptic and apoplectic forms a decidedly antiphlogistic treatment is necessary, such as free venesection, leeching, blisters, calomel, &c. Whereas, on the contrary, stimulants, anti-spasmodics, and sedatives are indicated in hysterical convulsions.

Epileptic convulsions, during labour, seem to depend very much upon irritation, caused by the presence of the fœtus *in utero*. Delivery, therefore, becomes an important remedial agent, provided the labour is sufficiently advanced to admit of it. The forceps is preferable to all other means of effecting delivery.

In epileptiform convulsions, chloroform inhalations have been found of great service in restraining the fits. But, according to the author's experience, a full dose of the hydrate of chloral by enema is still more effectual, especially if combined with bromide of potassium, as advised by Dr. Lusk, who remarks:—" It is my present practice, after beginning with chloroform, to administer thirty grains each of chloral and bromide of potassium by the rectum, and to suspend the chloroform so soon as the sedative effects of the latter agents become developed."*

From statistics of 35 cases of eclampsia occurring in his own practice, the author is led to the conclusion that the three principal remedies, in their order of importance, are bleeding, anæsthetics, and delivery.

Rupture of Uterus—Symptoms.

30. When a rupture of the uterus takes place during labour. The symptoms of this alarming accident are sudden and acute pain of the abdomen, followed by a ghastly pallor of the countenance, weak thready pulse, syncope, constant vomiting of dark grumous bloody fluid resembling coffee-grounds, and other signs of extreme prostration. There is usually a discharge of blood from the vagina. The presentation recedes out of reach, and, if the rent in the uterus be large, the child escapes through it into the abdominal cavity, where its limbs may be very distinctly felt through the parietes. In these cases, after sending for assistance, you may endeavour to keep up the powers of life by stimuli; but death nearly always takes place after a few hours.

Rupture of the uterus is the most dangerous complication of labour to which women are liable: it is fortunately rare, occurring about once in 1,331 cases. It may be occasioned by malpresentation, deformity of the pelvis, the abuse of ergot, awkward attempts to turn, or to use instruments, structural degenerations of the uterus, &c. In some instances, the rupture may not extend through the entire thickness of the uterine parietes. When it is of this partial character, it is attended with less imminent danger.

---

* Lusk's "Science and Art of Midwifery."

The vagina may be lacerated during labour at its junction with the uterus. The symptoms produced resemble those of ruptured uterus, but they are not so urgent, nor are they attended with so much danger.

When the uterus is ruptured, delivery should be accomplished as soon as possible, by turning, by the forceps, or by craniotomy.

If the child had escaped into the abdominal cavity, it was formerly considered necessary to pass the hand through the rent in the uterus in order to search for the feet, and then to deliver *per vias naturales;* but since the introduction of antiseptic surgery, it is now considered better practice to remove the fœtus by an incision through the abdominal parietes, and then to stitch up the rent in the uterus and to thoroughly cleanse the abdominal viscera by carbolized sponges before closing the external wound ; and certainly the results of modern practice tend to show that this operation, sometimes called "laparotomy," should be at once performed in all cases of extensive uterine rupture.

If the woman survive the immediate shock of the rupture, she will be likely to be carried off subsequently by peritonitis. Should peritonitis supervene, it must be treated in the usual way.

Thrombus of the Vulva—Symptoms.

31. In cases of thrombus or sanguineous tumour of the vagina or vulva. As the head, during labour, presses down on the plexus of vessels around the vaginal orifice, some of these may give way and cause a large subcutaneous effusion of blood. The occurrence of this accident is denoted by pain and tension in the part, and the sudden formation of a large tumour of a bluish colour, which is most frequently seated in one of the labia majora. It may become a serious im-

pediment to parturition, or may rupture and cause a dangerous hæmorrhage, or may terminate in gangrene.

Thrombus may occur during pregnancy, especially in the latter months, but is more usually a concomitant of labour, and arises in the manner just described. It is, however, a rare complication, and is dangerous in proportion to its size and severity and mode of termination, which may be either by resolution, suppuration, rupture, or gangrene.

The cervix uteri is sometimes the seat of thrombus during labour.

Treatment of Thrombus.

32. If the thrombus be large enough to impede delivery, a free incision will probably be necessary. You should therefore send for assistance, and in the meantime apply cold wet pads or a bladder of pounded ice to the part. Should the thrombus burst, and cause a copious hæmorrhage, which cannot be restrained by cold and pressure, the wound should be plugged with lint or a piece of sponge.

It is not advisable, according to Cazeaux, to open the tumour if it is small (being no larger, for example, than an egg), if the walls are of considerable thickness and of a natural colour, and if it is but slightly painful and does not increase in size.

Inversion of Uterus—Symptoms.

33. In cases of inversion of the uterus. This dangerous accident is rare. It usually happens very soon after the birth of the child. It may occur spontaneously, but much more frequently is the result of improper traction upon the cord when the placenta

is still attached. (See Note 36, Part I.) The inversion may be partial, and limited to the fundus; or the uterus may be turned completely inside out, and pass beyond the os externum, where it presents as a globular elastic tumour, with a bright red, rough, bleeding surface. As the uterus descends, the woman experiences a sensation as if a second child were coming into the world, and is immediately afterwards attacked with vomiting, syncope, and alarming prostration, accompanied, not unfrequently, with profuse hæmorrhage.

In complete inversion the uterus descends through the os uteri, until the whole organ becomes external to the vulva. The inverted organ then contains a cavity communicating with the abdomen, and lined by peritoneum. Within the cavity are the uterine appendages, and occasionally the intestine. In partial inversion, the fundus may be merely depressed into the cavity of the uterus, like the bottom of a glass bottle; or the greater portion of the uterus may be depressed, and form a tumour within the vagina, but not external. When the inversion is complete, no uterine tumour whatever can be felt in the hypogastric region; when it is partial, the depression of the fundus can often be felt through the parietes.

Inversion of the uterus is always attended with much peril. If the displacement be not speedily reduced, the woman will in all probability die from the immediate shock of the accident, or from hæmorrhage, inflammation, gangrene of the uterus, &c.

Inversion in some instances takes place spontaneously, in consequence of the woman making a sudden bearing-down effort immediately after the birth of the child.

Treatment of Inversion of Uterus.

34. When the uterus is inverted, you should send for assistance, but, at the same time, you should make

an immediate attempt to replace it. Accordingly, you compress the tumour firmly with both hands, and then push the fundus upwards into the pelvis, in the direction of the vaginal canal, by means of the fingers placed in the form of a cone. Should the placenta adhere to the uterus, it ought to be returned with it; but should it be impossible to do so, it may be separated. After the uterus is returned, the hand should be kept in its cavity until it is expelled, with the placenta, by the uterine contractions. Should the first attempt at reduction fail, you may try again, after emptying the bladder and rectum.

The reduction of an inverted uterus is comparatively easy, provided it be done immediately after the accident. The chief difficulty is felt in pushing the tumour past the perineum : as soon as it has passed this point, the uterus flies back into its proper position with a jerk.

If the uterus has been inverted for four or five hours, the reduction becomes exceedingly difficult, on account of the strangulation and consequent swelling of the inverted organ.

In all these operations chloroform is of the greatest service.

Retention of Placenta—Causes and Symptoms.

35. In cases of retention of the placenta. (See Note 36, Part I.) This may be due to three different causes, viz. : 1. Torpor of the uterus. 2. Irregular contraction. 3. Morbid adhesion of the placenta to the uterus. The symptoms of the first have already been mentioned (see 56, Part II.). In the second case there is a spasmodic or "hour-glass" contraction of some of the circular fibres, either of the os uteri internum (which is the most frequent), or of the body or fundus

of the uterus. The cord may be traced passing through the constriction. In the third case, the existence of adhesion can only be made out when the hand is introduced into the uterus in order to detach the placenta. In all these cases there will be much hæmorrhage if any portion of the placenta be detached.

The name "hour-glass contraction" has been given to irregular contraction of the uterus, because that organ appears to be divided into two chambers by the circular constriction of its fibres. The whole or only a portion of the placenta may be retained in the upper chamber. Irregular and spasmodic contraction of the uterus is very likely to ensue if the cord be dragged when the placenta is adherent. (See Note 36, Part I.)

Retained Placenta—Treatment.

36. When the placenta is retained, you must endeavour to excite the uterus to proper contractions by pressure and friction upon its surface. When there is uterine inertia, ergot of rye may also be given, as advised in Note 57, Part II. When the placenta is retained by irregular contraction, you may give a dose of opium, and keep up for some time gentle but steady traction upon the cord. However, in most of these cases, and especially when the placenta is morbidly adherent, the introduction of the hand into the uterus is the only measure which will suffice; but you had better not undertake this without a consultation.

When the hand is introduced into the uterus, the fingers are placed in a conical form, and gradually insinuated into the vagina. If there is hour-glass contraction, the cord serves as a guide along which the tips of the fingers are to be passed, until they reach the constriction. The tips of the fingers are then inserted into the stricture, and the fingers gradually and steadily expanded until they overcome the resistance of the circular uterine fibres. The hand can then be passed on into the uterine cavity, so as to remove the placenta. If the placenta be morbidly adherent, any detached portion of it should be seized, and the remainder gradually and cautiously separated by the fingers from the uterus until the whole can be removed. Whilst this is being done with one hand, the other hand should be placed externally on the abdomen, in order to grasp and steady the fundus uteri. These operations require much tact and delicacy. The introduction of the hand into the uterus is a measure always attended with some risk, but the operation becomes doubly hazardous when the placenta is morbidly adherent. There is then the danger of injuring the uterus, as well as of leaving portions of adherent placenta behind. These operations should never be attempted by the student, except in extreme cases; as, for instance, when there is a profuse hæmorrhage, and no assistance at hand. Should any portions of the placenta be left behind, they will be likely to decompose, and occasion much irritation. To obviate these effects the vagina should be syringed daily with weak disinfectant lotions. (See Note 69, Part II.)

Puerperal Fever—Symptoms.

37. In all cases of puerperal fever. These fevers assume various types and degrees, from the acutely inflammatory to the adynamic forms. From the inflammatory lesions, which are present in various cases, they have been called metro-peritonitis, hysteritis, uterine phlebitis, &c. The usual period of invasion is the third day after delivery. The more prominent symptoms in all cases are rigors, followed by severe headache, fever, high temperature, quick and often

feeble pulse, suppression of the milk and lochia, pain and tenderness on pressure in the uterine region, extending from thence over the whole abdomen. The woman loses all interest in her child, and her countenance betokens anxiety and great prostration of strength. Besides these symptoms, there are generally delirium, vomiting, tympanites abdominis, and sometimes diarrhœa. The disease usually ends in death after a few days.

There have been very great differences in the classifications of puerperal fevers. Dr. Lee referred them all to inflammation of different parts of the uterus and uterine appendages.

Dr. Ferguson believed them to depend upon a vitiation of the fluids from absorption of putrid matters, &c., by means of the inner surface of the uterus. In some of the worst forms of the disease no inflammatory lesions of any kind can be detected.

It is now generally admitted that the name "puerperal fever" has been given to a train of symptoms which are nearly always due to some kind of blood-poisoning or septicæmia. In some instances, which are called "autogenetic," the blood-poisoning originates with the patient herself, and is caused by the putrefaction of, and subsequent absorption from, retained portions of placenta, clots, shreds of membrane, lochial discharge, &c. In others, which are far more numerous, the poison has an external source; and it is well known that puerperal fever, in its worst form, is a highly contagious disease, and may be readily communicated from one patient to another, either directly or through the medium of the medical attendant. It has also been proved by numerous cases, that the disease may be produced by a variety of other animal poisons, but more especially by phlegmonous erysipelas and by scarlatina, to which last, indeed, Dr. Braxton Hicks refers the greater number of cases which he has collected. It was ascertained, moreover, by Dr. Semelweiss, at the Vienna Lying-in

Hospital, in 1846, that puerperal fever could frequently be traced to examinations made by students who had, just before, been engaged in opening bodies in the dead-house; and, in consequence, a rule was made, which was attended with the best results, that every student who had been so engaged should wash his hands in chlorinated water before examining a lying-in patient.

It cannot, therefore, be too strongly impressed on the minds of students that the greatest caution is necessary in order to avoid communicating the disease. No medical man should go to a labour for at least a week after seeing a case of puerperal fever; and when he does go, he should take care that he has on no single article of dress which he wore on that occasion. If he has had two consecutive cases of the disease, he ought to give up midwifery practice for some weeks. No student should go to a labour after dressing an erysipelatous patient or making a post-mortem examination, especially of a case of abdominal inflammation. It is better, indeed, that students should not attend midwifery cases whilst they are engaged as dressers at hospitals.

Dr. Schroeder has well remarked that "the accoucheur must consider his hands not quite free from poison if he has handled any portion of a dead body; if he has seen a patient suffering from phlegmonous erysipelas or any kind of pyæmia; if he has dressed suppurating or diphtheric wounds; if he has come in contact with decomposing new growths; if (in the case of abortion) he has extracted a decomposed ovum or portions of it; if he has examined women with badly smelling lochia or suffering from puerperal fever. He must then cleanse his hands most scrupulously before he undertakes the examination of a parturient or puerperal woman;" and then he must use the strictest antiseptic precautions also. (See 90, Part II.)

It is scarcely necessary to add that every conscientious accoucheur will be scrupulously clean in his person and habits. To no class of men does the saying, "Cleanliness is next to godliness," apply so forcibly.

The author is in the habit of using the Turkish bath after he has been exposed to infection of any kind, and he can confidently recommend it as the best means of cleansing the skin and eliminating animal poisons from the system.

Puerperal fever may commence within twenty-four hours after delivery. The most usual period of invasion, however, is from forty-eight to seventy-two hours. Again, it may not come on until five or six days afterwards.

The pulse averages, in most cases, from 120 to 140 beats in a minute, but it may rise to 160. It is usually small and feeble, but in the more sthenic forms is hard and wiry. The temperature is usually as much as 104° or 105°.

The countenance in puerperal fever is very characteristic, and very soon assumes the Hippocratic character. The complexion is pale and sallow, with a hectic patch in the centre of the cheek.

The treatment is nearly always unsatisfactory, and appears to have little effect in delaying the fatal termination. The cases most amenable to treatment are the more acute forms of peritonitis, which come on soon after a severe or instrumental labour, for instance. These bear more resemblance to ordinary peritonitis, and require much the same treatment, viz., (sometimes) bleeding, leeches, mercury to affect the system, opiates, and warm fomentations. These are the cases which are most likely to recover.

A somewhat different treatment is required in what is called the gastro-bilious puerperal fever (puerperal intestinal irritation of Locock). Here, free purgation, by castor oil, calomel, and enemata, is necessary.

The form called uterine phlebitis is best treated by leeches, cataplasms, Dover's powder, and calomel to affect the system. The vagina should be syringed out daily, as recommended in Note 69, Part II. This is a most useful measure in all cases of puerperal fever.

The adynamic form, or puerperal fever "par excellence," is the scourge of lying-in hospitals; being at the same time the most contagious, and the least amenable to treatment. In this form there are sometimes no morbid appearances to be found after death in the uterus or its appendages. In other instances, signs of inflammation are observed, and occasionally purulent deposits are met with in the joints, orbits, &c., as in cases of pyæmia. It appears to make very little difference in the result, whether a stimulant or antiphlogistic plan of treatment be adopted. The remedies usually adopted are calomel and opium in repeated doses; quinine in five-grain doses twice or three times a day; turpentine, both internally and as an external application to the abdomen; sometimes, in excep tional cases, leeches. Nourishing broths, wine, and other stimuli are always necessary to sustain the vital powers.

Phlegmasia Dolens—Symptoms.

38. In cases of phlegmasia dolens. This disease usually comes on about ten days or a fortnight after delivery. It sets in with rigors, headache, quick pulse, restlessness, and general *malaise*. These are speedily followed by pain and tenderness in the hypogastrium or groin, extending down the thigh and leg of that side; the whole limb then becomes greatly enlarged, immovable, and at the same time hot, tense, elastic, white, and shining. The femoral veins and lymphatics are hard, knotted, and tender to the touch. There is much accompanying constitutional irritation, feverishness, and want of sleep. The pulse may reach 120, and the temperature 101° or 102°, especially in the evening. The tongue is furred, the face is pallid, the milk and lochia usually much diminished. These symptoms commonly pass off in two or three weeks, but the limb may remain stiff and lame for a much longer period.

There has been much discussion at various times as to the pathology of phlegmasia dolens, or "white leg," as it is vulgarly called. It now seems pretty well established that the disease consists in an inflammation and obstruction of the principal veins, and also lymphatics, of the limb affected; and this inflammation, in most instances, is due to the imbibition of poison by the uterine veins.

The pain and swelling do not always progress from above downwards. The disease sometimes commences in the calf of the leg, which is the seat of a violent cramp-like pain, speedily succeeded by swelling.

The limb affected may increase to at least double its ordinary size. The swelling is so firm and elastic, that it very seldom pits on pressure, and is scarcely influenced in any way by position.

It occasionally happens, that as soon as the disease has abated in one leg, the other is attacked, and goes through a similar course, except that the symptoms are scarcely ever so severe. In some rare cases both legs are attacked at once.

In the treatment of this disease, if the symptoms of local inflammation are very marked, leeches may be applied with advantage, and afterwards poultices. In general, however, they will not be required, and it will be sufficient at first to envelope the whole limb in cotton-wool and oiled silk or sheet gutta-percha. If there is much pain, opiates and poppy-head fomentations will give great relief. After two or three days, turpentine stupes or blisters to the affected part are very useful. When the acute stage is past, tonics, especially the preparations of iron, are proper, together with a generous diet. The affected limb may then be painted with iodine, or rubbed with various stimulating liniments, and afterwards enveloped in a flannel bandage.

Phlegmasia dolens rarely goes on to a fatal termination. Should it end thus, the disease in all probability has either accompanied uterine phlebitis, or has resulted in an attack of general phlebitis, followed by deposits of pus in various remote parts of the body.

Puerperal Thrombosis and Embolia—Symptoms.

39. In cases of threatened syncope from puerperal thrombosis. In women who have been lately delivered

(especially when there has been hæmorrhage from inefficient uterine contraction after labour), the sudden occurrence of dyspnœa, palpitation, and syncope is an alarming symptom, because it usually denotes an altered condition of the blood, which has led to the formation of clots, and consequent obstruction of the pulmonary circulation.

The pathology of puerperal thrombosis and embolia has been very well explained by Dr. R. Barnes, in a paper which was published in the "Obstetrical Transactions" for 1863. It is thus described :—
"1. There is a dyscrasia of the blood immediately proceeding from the puerperal process, which is favourable to the production of clots in the uterine veins and veins of the lower extremities. Imperfect contraction of the uterus, the formation of putrilage in the uterine cavity from the admission of air, which acts upon the blood and serum squeezed out of the vessels, and the remains of adherent placenta or of decidua, are often the immediate antecedent conditions of peripheral thrombosis. . . . .
"2. The next step is that of embolia. Portions of the peripheral thrombi, attended, no doubt, in many cases, by septic matter derived from the uterus, are carried to the right heart. If the solid matters be large enough, or the septic or ichorous matters be irritating enough, to cause a violent perturbation of the heart's action, and to act chemically on the blood-mass, rapid coagulation of blood in the right cavities may ensue, followed by a similar process in the larger pulmonary arteries. In such cases sudden death occurs.
"3. But in those cases in which either minute portions of thrombi are taken up from the peripheral veins, or when the septic or ichorous matter is less virulent, no clot may form in the right heart, but minute emboli may be carried into the finer divisions of the pulmonary artery, causing lobular pneumonia, ending in slower death, or possibly in recovery.

"4. It has been noticed that in many of these cases some mental emotion or sudden exertion has immediately preceded (and has seemed to be the exciting cause of) the cardiac and pulmonic distress."

With respect to the treatment of these cases, Dr. Barnes states:—"The point of first importance is to encourage lactation." "The next points are, to enforce the recumbent position; to remove all causes of mental or bodily disturbance; not to starve the patient, and thus to give activity to the absorption of foul matters, but to supply the circulating fluid with generous materials."

The remedies adapted to these cases are stimuli and tonics; wine, bark, iron, and especially ammonia, which, besides being a stimulant, is also believed, in accordance with Dr. Richardson's views, to have a powerful solvent action upon any clots which may have formed in the heart or blood-vessels.

Pelvic Cellulitis and Abscess.

40. In cases of pelvic cellulitis* and abscess. This affection comes on insidiously some two or three weeks after delivery or abortion. It is denoted by fixed pain, swelling, and tenderness, just above the pelvic brim in one iliac region or groin; by hardness and tenderness, on vaginal examination, in the neighbourhood of the os uteri; and by painful micturition and defæcation. There is much accompanying general disturbance, quick pulse, hectic fever, and loss of appetite. Suppuration is denoted by rigors and increased severity of the local tenderness and throbbing. The pus may be

---

* Called by Virchow "Parametritis."

discharged externally above Poupart's ligament, or into the vagina, rectum, or bladder. This event usually gives relief to all the symptoms.

In this affection the inflammatory effusion appears to be the result of absorption of irritant matters from the uterine surface. The actual seat of the effusion is usually the meshes of the areolar tissue surrounding the uterus, between the folds of the broad ligament; but in some cases there is probably pelvic peritonitis present.

The abscess most frequently bursts into the vagina, rectum, or bladder, and the case terminates favourably. Sometimes, however, it escapes externally, after burrowing and forming troublesome sinuses, which cause the recovery to be very protracted. In some rare instances it has been known to give way into the peritoneal cavity, and prove rapidly fatal.

The treatment consists in topical depletion by leeches, warm fomentations, poultices, and turpentine stupes. The pain and restlessness at night should be relieved by opiates and hydrate of chloral, or by opiate enemata and belladonna pessaries. Tonics and a nutritious diet are required, especially towards the termination. When distinct fluctuation can be perceived, either externally or in the vagina, the abscess may be opened; but as this operation requires considerable tact and discrimination, a consultation should be requested.

Puerperal Mania—Symptoms.

41. In cases of puerperal mania. This form of insanity may show itself as acute mania, or assume the more chronic form, melancholia. The first kind commences very soon after labour; the pulse continues very frequent, and the excitement of the second stage, instead of abating, increases to a wild delirium, which, if not relieved, may end in coma, paralysis, and death.

The second kind usually commences two or three days after labour, when the flow of milk sets in, or at a still later period; and is very apt to assume the form of religious melancholy. The patient is captious, suspicious, and liable to take sudden and unaccountable aversions to those about her. There is often a total want of sleep; the bowels are usually constipated, and the secretions much vitiated. If fever be present, it is of a low form, and there is a general want of power in the system.

When the acute form of puerperal mania terminates fatally, the *post-mortem* appearances usually found are—thickening and opacity of the cerebral membranes, together with vascularity, softening, and effusions of blood or serum in the brain or membranes. This form appears in some instances to be nothing more than a particular kind of puerperal fever. In the chronic form there is usually headache, offensive breath, a sunken appearance of the eye, and pallor or sallowness of the countenance. If there is any accompanying fever it is of a low type. This kind appears to be mostly connected with derangement of the digestive organs. In other instances it has been clearly traceable to exhaustion, arising from profuse hæmorrhage during labour, or from over-lactation. In other instances, again, it would appear to have a toxæmic origin, as evinced by the presence of albumen in the urine, &c. In the first kind of puerperal mania, an antiphlogistic treatment is proper, such as leeches, and cold to the head, warm pediluvia, and smart purgatives. In the other kinds, purgatives are necessary; and afterwards great attention should be paid to diet, and to the regulation of the bowels. In all, should sleep be absent, sedatives will be required; but for this purpose hydrate of chloral is preferable to opium, which often tends to increase the cerebral excitement. Hydrate of chloral should be given in full doses of from thirty to sixty grains, and it is a good plan to combine it with camphor. Dr. Lusk prefers an enema containing hydrate of chloral and bromide of potassium āā gr. xxx. In those cases which appear to be the result of exhausting discharges, the patient should be put on a generous diet and a course of tonics. Sedatives are also of much service. If over-lactation appear to be the cause, the child must be weaned.

INDEX.

	PAGE
Abortion, diagnosis of	38
treatment of	38
with retention of part of the ovum	106
with profuse hæmorrhage	106
After-pains	83
Antiseptic midwifery	104
Arrest of head in pelvis	117
Artificial respiration	75
Ascites of fœtus	124
Asphyxia of infant	74
treatment of	74
Athill, Dr., on warm water injections in post-partum hæmorrhage	81
Bandage after labour	30
Barnes, Dr., on puerperal thrombosis	146
on injections in post-partum hæmorrhage	81
Bed during labour, how to guard	15
Belladonna, use of, as an anti-lactescent	96
Breasts, inflammation of	98
treatment of	99
Breech presentations, mechanism of	54
diagnosis of	56
evils of early interference in	57
management of	57
arrest of body in	121
arrest of head in	121
Brow presentation	118

INDEX.

	PAGE
Calculus in bladder during labour	114
Catheterism during labour	69
Cellulitis, pelvic	147
Chloroform, inhalation of, during labour	45
mode of administering	46
Champneys, Dr., on expulsion of placenta	25, 28
Churchill, Dr., statistics of first stage	42
presentations	52
on the pulse after labour	77
Colostrum	34
Convulsions, epileptic	130
hysterical	132
apoplectic	132
treatment of	132
Cord, umbilical, *see* Funis.	
Cramps during labour	70
Credè's method of "expressing" the placenta	26
Death of fœtus	70
signs of	71
labour after	70
Deformities of pelvis	115
Delay in expulsion of body	73
Diet during labour	14
after labour	35
Duncan, Dr. Matthews, on expulsion of placenta	28
Ephemeral fever	101
Ergot of rye	42
Ergotin, hypodermic injection of	80
Extension, movement of	19
Extra-uterine pregnancy	107
Face presentation, mechanism of	52
diagnosis of	52
management of	54

INDEX.

	PAGE
Ferguson, Dr., on puerperal fever	141
Fever, puerperal	140
treatment of	143
Fillet in breech presentations	121
Flooding, *see* Hæmorrhage.	
Fœtus, death of	70
viability of	38
Foot presentations	61
diagnosis of	61
management of	62
Funis, ligature and division of	23
bandaging of	30
coiling of, round neck	72
prolapse of	125
Gooch, Dr., rules for leaving during labour	11
on post-partum hæmorrhage	77
Hæmorrhage after delivery	77
symptoms of	78
treatment of	78
internal	82
secondary	90
accidental	126
unavoidable	128
Hall, Dr. M., on the cold douche	80
method of performing artificial respiration	76
Head, rotation of	19
expulsion of	21
interval after birth of	21
Hewitt, Dr. Graily, on support of the perineum	21
Hydrocephalus	124
Imperforate os uteri	113
Incontinence of urine after delivery	87
Inertia of uterus in twin cases	67

154 INDEX.

	PAGE
Instruments, &c., required during labour	1
Inversion of uterus	136
treatment of	137
Involution of the womb	36
Iodide of potassium as an anti-lactescent	96
King, Dr., on treatment of placenta prævia	130
Knee presentations, diagnosis of	62
management of	62
Labour, signs of commencing	7
premonitory signs of	7
first stage of	7
prompt attention to	1
preliminary observations of	2
prognosis of	12
second stage of	14
third stage of	24
diet during	14
diet after	35
questions during	2
mode of ascertaining progress of	13
repose after	31
premature	39
tedious, causes of	41
from loaded rectum	41
from inefficient uterine action	42
from want of sleep	43
from rigid os uteri	43
from premature rupture of membranes	44
from œdematous os uteri	44
from toughness of membranes	44
from rigid soft parts	46
from unfavourable presentations	47
from want of room	68
powerless	112
Lee, Dr., on puerperal fever	141

	PAGE
Lochial discharge	35
deficiency of	88
excessive	88
offensive	89
Lusk, Dr., on the attitude of medical attendant	3
on treatment of puerperal mania	150
on treatment of puerperal convulsions	133
McClintock, Dr., on removal of placenta	27
Mania, puerperal	148
Membranes, rupture of	16
how to remove	28
Merriman, Dr., on twin cases	65
Miliary fever	102
Milk, secretion of	34
substitute for	34
how to get rid of	95
fever	100
treatment of	101
Mole pregnancy	108
Nervous shock	84
treatment of	85
Nipples, retracted	96
sore	97
Ophthalmia, purulent, of infants	103
treatment of	104
Os uteri, state of, in first stage	7
in second stage	16
in primiparæ and in multiparæ	9
how to distinguish	9
rigid	43
imperforate	113
Pains, spurious, diagnosis of	40
treatment of	40

INDEX.

	PAGE
Parametritis	147
Paralysis of legs after labour	94
Patient, during labour, when to leave	11
time for leaving, after labour	31
visits to, after labour	33
inquiries respecting	33
management of	36
Pelvic cellulitis and abscess	147
tumours	114
Pelvis, deformities of	115
Perineum, support of	20
laceration of	92
treatment of	92
Phlegmasia dolens	144
Placenta, expulsion of	24
danger of forcibly detaching	26
how to ascertain detachment of	27
how to aid expulsion of	26
battledore	27
how to remove	27
examination of, after removal	29
retention of	138
retained, treatment of	139
prævia, diagnosis of	128
treatment of	129
Playfair, Dr., on lotion for abraded nipples	98
Position during first stage	13
Powerless labour	112
Pregnancy, diagnosis of	37
Presentation, diagnosis of	9
head, signs of	10
ordinary	16
forehead, anteriorly	47
diagnosis	47
mechanism	50
face	52
breech	54

INDEX. 157

	PAGE
Presentation, brow	118
where none can be felt	118
upper extremity	122
placenta	128
foot	61
knee	62
compound	63
hand with head	63
hand with breech or foot	64
Prognosis in natural labour	12
Prolapse of bladder during labour	115
of funis	125
Prolapsus uteri	93
Puerperal convulsions	130
fever	140
treatment of	143
mania	148
thrombosis	145
Purgative after delivery	34
Ramsbotham, Dr., on occipito-posterior presentations	49
Rest after delivery, use of	32
Restitution, movement of	21
Retention of urine during labour	69
after labour	86
of placenta	138
treatment of	139
Retroversion of the gravid uterus	109
diagnosis of	110
treatment of	111
Rigby, Dr., on post-partum hæmorrhage	80
on pelvic deformity	116
Rigors after labour	29
Rotation, movement of	19
Rupture of uterus	134
Scalp, tumour of	16

158 INDEX.

	PAGE
Schroeder, Dr., on temperature after labour	32
on prophylaxis of puerperal fever	142
Shoulders, rotation of	22
presentation of	122
Silvester, Dr., method of performing artificial respiration	76
Simpson, Sir J. Y., on detachment of placenta prævia	130
Sleeplessness after delivery	86
Smith, Dr. Tyler, on treatment of post-partum hæmorrhage	81
Spiegelberg on management of third stage of labour	25
on examination of placenta	29
Stage, first, signs of	7
pains during	8
position during	13
second, signs of	14
position during	14
management of	18
third, duration of	25
Strictures of vagina	113
Tedious labour from want of room	68
Temperature after delivery	32
in mammary abscess	99
in puerperal fever	143
Thrombus of vulva—symptoms	135
treatment	136
Tumours in pelvis	114
Twin births, mechanism of	65
diagnosis of	65
management of	66
Uterus, state of, during third stage	25
after expulsion of the placenta	29
prolapse of	93
rupture of	134
inversion of	136
treatment of	137

	PAGE
Vagina, how to syringe	89
normal state of	6
strictures of	113
state of, in second stage	16
Vaginal examinations, how to make	4
when to make	5
information derived from	5
frequency of	13
Vienna Hospital, precautions in	141
Virchow on parametritis	147
Vomiting during labour	40
Weid	101

www.ingramcontent.com/pod-product-compliance
Lightning Source LLC
Chambersburg PA
CBHW030245170426
43202CB00009B/627